THE STORY OF BRITAIN

RICHARD GARRETT

GRANADA
London Toronto Sydney New York

Editor
Jilly Glassborow

Design
Tom Deas

Cartographer
Malcolm Porter

Illustrators
Frederick St. Ward
Shirley Willis

To Sarah

Published by Granada Publishing 1983
Granada Publishing Limited
Frogmore, St Albans, Herts AL2 2NF

36 Golden Square, London W1R 4AH
866 United Nations Plaza, New York, NY 10017, USA
117 York Street, Sydney, NSW 2000, Australia
60 International Blvd, Rexdale, Ontario R9W 6J2, Canada
61 Beach Road, Auckland, New Zealand

Copyright © Richard Garrett
Illustrations copyright © Granada Publishing

British Library Cataloguing in Publication Data
Garrett, Richard
The story of Britain
1. Great Britain—History
I. Title
941   DA30
ISBN 0-246-12040-1

Printed in Italy by New Interlitho

Granada ®
Granada Publishing ®

Contents

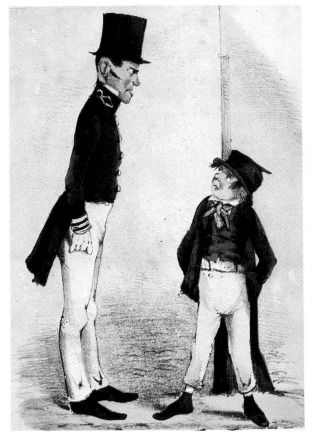

The Making of Britain

*From the time Man first appeared in Britain
over a quarter of a million years ago, wave upon
wave of invaders from overseas raided and then settled
the land. But with the Norman Conquest in 1066 all
this was to change. Britain was never again
successfully invaded by any other nation.*

Britain is Born

Six thousand million years ago our solar system was born. The planets were created, and there was Earth. For millions of years, the surface of the Earth underwent changes. Europe was joined to North America; Britain to Europe. The present North Sea was once a scorching desert. Later, it became a vast forest. There were volcanoes to the north-east of Scotland.

The first part of Britain to emerge from the sea was a chain of small islands. Today, they are the peaks of mountains in the Highlands and Western Isles of Scotland. As the pattern became clearer, volcanoes tore the land apart and reshaped it. The earth folded itself into creases. Eventually, they became hills and valleys. The granite of Cornwall was created by the red hot flow of lava. Elsewhere, there were huge forests and sweltering swamps.

At intervals there were four long periods of cold. They were called the Ice Ages. We shall never know anything like them. The glaciers came from the north until they reached the edge of what is now London. But, in between each Ice

Age, the climate was quite warm.

Just as the shape of the land changed, so did the creatures that inhabited it. At one time, there were monsters such as dinosaurs (massive lizards with tiny heads) and pterodactyls (flying reptiles). Sabre-toothed tigers roamed in what is now the Thames valley. Later, during the Ice Ages, there were elephants and rhinoceroses. But, because it was so cold, they had long and shaggy fur coats.

The First People

Half a million years ago, there were man-like creatures roaming the earth. They were probably able to make and use stone implements; they almost certainly knew how to build fires. According to one estimate, there were about two hundred of them in Britain.

Two hundred and fifty thousand years later, these ancestors of present day man had become more recognizably members of our own species. We know this from pieces of a human skull that were discovered in a quarry at Swanscombe in Kent one day in 1936. Some fragments of flint were also found. They had probably been used as axes.

How did these people from the early morning of history live? They moved from one forest clearing to the next; from one cave to another. Life was a never ending search for food. They hunted the woolly rhino, the mastodon (a hairy elephant) and wild horses. For the rest of their diet, they lived off roots, berries and insects. By trial and error, they discovered what was poisonous, and what was not. When there was no other meat, they probably became cannibals. They manufactured their weapons by chipping bits off large lumps of stone. Somehow they communicated with one another by signs and grunts. They could not speak, for they had no language.

Britain, still joined to Europe, was visited by

Left: Between the Ice Ages, the climate of Britain was quite mild. Giant elephants and wild horses roamed the Thames valley. In modern times, the remains of a man have been discovered at Swanscombe in Kent. Experts say they are 200,000 years old.

Right: Avebury Ring in Wiltshire was probably built between 2000 and 1600BC. It may have been connected with Bronze Age religious rites.

The Prehistoric Man Who Wasn't
In 1912, a solicitor named Charles Dawson claimed to have dug up the remains of a prehistoric man near the Sussex village of Piltdown. There was the brain case of a human skull; a jawbone with teeth in it; and some flint instruments. Dawson suggested that this stranger from the past was 250,000 years old – a left-over from an Ice Age. At first, even the experts believed him. But in 1953 – long after Dawson had died – it was established that the brain case was about 50,000 years old. The jaw bone and the teeth, however, had belonged to an ape. As for the flints, they had been dug up near the town of Bizerta in Tunisia. The whole thing was an elaborate hoax.

parties of hunters from elsewhere. They, too, explored the heathlands and the forests, searching for food. In about 20,000 BC the last of the Ice Ages began to melt away. In the wake of the cold, enormous pine forests grew up. No sun shone in these places; there was very little game to be found.

At last – by about 12,000 BC – the ice finally receded. People were now learning how to make tools and weapons from bones as well as flints; to cover their nakedness with skins. They even carved female figures from stone, which had, or so they believed, the power of magic. What was

Our ancient ancestors were hunters, but soon they were fighting one another. They discovered that weapons, such as these battle axes (1800–1400BC), were very useful.

more important, people had now learned how to speak.

Roughly 5000 years ago the land link with Europe was broken. The Straits of Dover were created, and the pines began to yield to deciduous trees such as oaks. It had taken a long, long time; but so many things now became possible. Men chopped down trees, cleared space in the forests and learned how to grow crops. They kept cattle and pigs – in Scotland, sheep. They dug mines from which to quarry flint. And they built homes.

The home was a hut, nearly always circular. The floor was sunk beneath ground level; a pole in the middle supported the roof. When two or three or four of these crude cottages were built in one area, the result was a village. Many villages had small forts, built from earth, as defences. Work on the largest, Maiden Castle in Dorset, was begun in the year 3000 BC.

The Early Settlers

About 2000 years before Christ, a race of people came to Britain from the estuaries of Northern Europe. They were known as the Beaker Folk, after the clay mugs (beakers) they used to make. But their most important achievement was the art of manufacturing tools and ornaments from bronze.

Bronze is made from a mixture of copper and tin. The tin came from Cornwall; copper from the mountains of Ireland. To bring the two together meant a lot of travelling.

In the Wicklow Hills of Ireland, they had found gold. The men who mined it were artists. They transformed it into ear-rings, bracelets and necklets. On their journeys to obtain copper, the Beaker Folk used to bring these trinkets back to England with them.

People were now travelling considerable distances. They exchanged ideas and traded with one another; bartering this for that – pleased that others wanted their own goods, and excited about new discoveries. They had learned how to build and sail ships. Visitors from the Continent crossed the English Channel to the small natural harbours on the south and east coasts. Larger vessels came from the Mediterranean. There were voyages along the edge of the Atlantic, where the great waves gather themselves up and hurl themselves at the shores.

Although they could not write, the Beaker Folk had a religion. Today, there are traces of it in circles of stones at places as far apart as the Orkneys, the Midlands, and on the moors of Devonshire. The greatest of them all was Stonehenge in Wiltshire.

The Beaker Folk were buried on the edges of settlements: each in his own grave – with his beaker for drinks after death, and an arrow head in case he might need it.

A Place of Worship

The dead as well as the living had homes. The earliest burial places were on the edges of settlements. The corpses were placed in an inner chamber with a stone roof and walls. When it was full, the entrance was sealed up by a large slab. But the Beaker Folk believed that the dead should be buried individually – each in a crouching position, and clasping his or her drinking pot (presumably to take light refreshments on the other side of life).

Circles of standing stones in lonely places mark their graves. If you come across them unexpectedly out of the mist, they produce a feeling of awe – as though they are touched by magic. No doubt they were also used for worship, but the nature of the worship remains a mystery.

Without a doubt, the most magnificent of these strange, haunted, places is Stonehenge on Salisbury Plain. There are many signs to show that Beaker Folk were buried round the edge of it. But the large stones in the centre had some other purpose. They are arranged in such a way that they can indicate the summer solstice and even predict the eclipse of the moon. Perhaps they were a kind of enormous calendar that mapped the progress of the year. Perhaps, too, they gave priests the power to make prophecies.

Stonehenge was built in three phases between 1800 and 1400 BC. The Beaker people certainly had a hand in it, for carvings in bronze – showing axe heads and a dagger – have been discovered. Beyond this, however, we can only guess. The mystery of Stonehenge is as unyielding as the huge stones from which it was built.

Eighty-two of the larger stones used in the construction of Stonehenge are known to have come from the Prescelly Mountains in south-west Wales. The mystery is how, 3000 years ago, these massive slabs were transported all the way to Wiltshire. By sledges and rafts? Possibly. It was certainly a vast undertaking for a primitive civilisation.

This ornament for the neck of an elegant Iron Age citizen was made from an alloy of gold and silver – about the 1st century BC.

Celtic Britain

Compared to countries bordering the Mediterranean and in Asia Minor, the development of Britain was slow. The first pyramid had been built in Egypt one thousand years before the construction of Stonehenge. By 2500 BC Babylonian merchants could not only write; they actually made maps of their estates.

In every way, the people from this sunnier part of the world were more advanced. When one ancient Briton was quarrelling (and doubtless fighting) with another about the right to a patch of land, the Egyptians were conducting organized wars.

We don't know whether the Beaker Folk fought amongst themselves. We can be certain, however, that the Celts – who arrived 1500 years later – were very warlike. They came from France and the low countries – at first in small numbers, later in hordes. They were tall men: strong and muscular with fair complexions. They were high spirited, excitable, and when they were not fighting, they enjoyed feasting.

With the Celts came a new language. You can still hear traces of it in Cornwall, Ireland, and Wales, and in the north-west of Scotland.

The Celtic priests (called Druids) taught new ideas about immortality and the Universe. Their craftsmen introduced a new metal to the islands – iron.

Iron was more useful than bronze. It was harder, and you did not have to search for two ingredients (copper and tin) in the mountains. The first deposits of iron ore were probably discovered in the Forest of Dean and in the Kent and Sussex Weald.

The most warlike of the Celtic tribes was the Belgae who came from the Low Countries (of which Belgium is a part). They had their own king, and they were nearly always in the spearhead of the Celtic advance as it spread across Britain. Gradually they penetrated into Scotland, to Wales and into Cornwall.

If the inhabitants of Britain meekly gave them what they wanted, there was no trouble. Some of them married local girls and settled down. But if anyone attempted to resist, fighting broke out.

Warfare cannot have come as a complete surprise to the British. There were already hill forts scattered over the country. But these defences were not enough to keep away the Celts. Many of the tribesmen had already experienced fighting in Europe. They were led by warrior chiefs; armed with iron swords and daggers.

A Celtic chief had a chariot, though it seems doubtful whether he used it in battle. It may have been just for display; it was certainly buried with him when he died.

The simple natives of Britain stood little chance against such tough and well armed invaders. Wherever the Celts went, they conquered. To make sure they held on to the captured land, they, too, built forts, sturdy earthworks reinforced with timber.

But not all their land had to be taken from the British. Parts of the country had never been settled. The forests, in particular, were left alone, for people were afraid of them and communities preferred the high ground. The fearless Belgae, however, decided to occupy the south-east of England, which was thick with trees. They cut down the timber and cleared the soil. It was well worth the trouble. The crops turned out to be far better than those grown on the bleak upland fields.

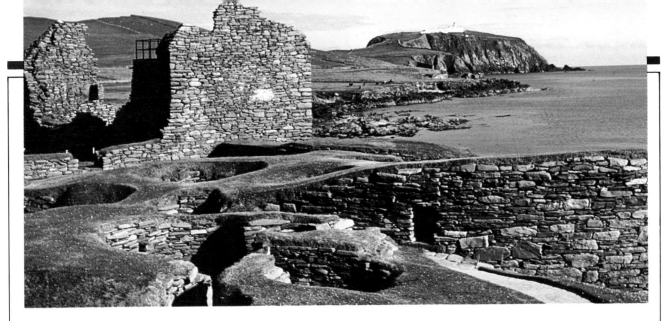

The remains of Bronze and Iron Age settlements in the Shetland Islands. They may have been simple, but they were refuge against the fierce weather and enemy attack.

Early Village Life

Until the arrival of the Celts, there were no permanent homes. As the seasons changed, a man and his family moved on with their livestock in search of better grazing land. The valleys were thick with trees. Wolves, bears and lynxes still roamed in these dark places.

It was better to keep to the higher ground: to the moors and the downland, where there was grass for the animals, and where a crop of barley could be grown from the thin soil. To till this soil, they used a kind of plough. The earliest examples of these instruments were hand-held spikes that bit into the earth. A man would work over his land twice – on the second occasion, moving at right angles to the first.

During the Stone Age – from about 3000 BC – man learned how to build a more permanent home. The roof was thatched; the floor was sunk beneath the ground. A fire provided warmth, but there was no chimney. The smoke escaped through the entrance, and gaps in the walls.

The appearances of these early houses varied from one part of Britain to another. In the North of Scotland, for example, there were plenty of stones, and these were used to build them. They were similar to larger constructions (some of them over six metres high) known as 'brochs', which were used as shelters against sudden attack. Since there were fewer stones in Southern Scotland, the inhabitants made round huts from mud.

The early inhabitants of Ireland made themselves huts that looked rather like giant beehives.

The walls were made of stone; the roofs put together from reeds. During winter nights, families huddled over peat fires that smouldered in the centres of the earthen floors.

As time went by and the Celts arrived, the newcomers laid out large rectangular fields. They marked the boundaries either by ditches or else (as, for instance, in Cornwall) by drystone walls. They also improved the method of ploughing. They produced wooden blades with iron tips, and used oxen to haul them. Having gone to so much trouble, they saw no point in moving on as the seasons changed. The farms and villages they built became permanent.

Gradually a system of tracks spread across the country. Each linked one community with another; they usually followed the edges of the high ground. Where they had to cross marshland, causeways of split logs and brushwood were built.

Many of the settlers now lived in houses that had one circular wall within another. The family inhabited the smaller; the sheep and cattle were given shelter within the outer.

The men of the village looked after the animals and ploughed the fields. The women wove cloth from which they made garments; manufactured cooking pots from clay; and ground the corn.

Every village had a smith, who smelted the iron ore and wrought it into tools and weapons. Sometimes, a wandering trader called – offering beads from Egypt, amber from the Baltic, or golden ornaments from Ireland. From these visitors, the simple farming community received its only news of the great world beyond.

People died. From the middle of the Bronze Age, the dead were cremated. The ceremony normally took place on the edge of a hill. Afterwards, the burnt bones (still hot) were placed inside an urn, which was covered by a circular mound.

The Roman Conquest

By 60 BC, the Romans had conquered much of the land around the Mediterranean. One great general named Julius Caesar had overrun nearly all France, but had experienced a lot of trouble from the Belgae. They were, he knew, receiving help from their kinsmen in Britain. There was only one thing for it: Britain would have to be invaded.

On the morning of 25 August, 55 BC, a fleet of eighty transports escorted by war galleys sailed from a point on the French coast near Boulogne. At 10 AM, the ships reached the shores of Kent between Deal and Walmer.

On board the transports, packed shoulder to shoulder, were 10,200 men of the 7th and 10th Legions. Somewhere out at sea, there were eighteen more vessels with 240 cavalrymen and their horses on board, but there was no sign of them. The captains had made a disastrous mistake. They had misjudged the tides. The horse soldiers never turned up.

Caesar, too, had made a mistake. Despite his battles against the Belgae in Europe, he had under-rated their military strength in Britain. As the Roman soldiers saw them waiting on the beach, led by their king, Cassivelaunus, they hesitated. Nobody seemed anxious to go ashore.

Eventually, the standard bearer of the 10th Legion jumped into the surf and urged the men to follow him. Minutes later, the fight began.

It was not Caesar's day. The opposition was much tougher than he had expected, and heavy casualties were piling up in his ranks. To make matters worse, the weather was getting bad, and a number of ships were wrecked on the shore. Prudently, Caesar decided to withdraw. The conquest of Britain would have to wait.

Next year, he came again with a much larger force. The weather for the crossing was fine. Five legions and two thousand cavalrymen came ashore. Three more legions and more horse soldiers waited off the coast in reserve.

Over the Channel, the clouds were massing for what promised to be another storm. This time, Caesar ignored the threat. Some of the ships were hauled ashore and earthworks hastily dug up around them. They served as forts to protect the beach head.

Cassivelaunus's men were fighting desperately, but there was little they could do against such a well armed and disciplined enemy. The Romans broke through. They marched as far as Wheathampstead in Hertfordshire, where they fought another battle. But Cassivelaunus had had enough. He surrendered, agreed to pay taxes to Rome and to hand over hostages.

His purpose accomplished, Caesar withdrew to the Kent coast. He re-embarked his army, and set sail back to France. For the better part of one hundred years, there were no more visits by Roman soldiers to Britain.

The Roman Soldier

The backbone of the Roman army was its infantry – the legionaries, as they were called. They were armed with light spears, swords and daggers. The officers wore metal breast- and back-plates; the common soldiers had to be content with leather. Each man had a shield.

A man served in a legion for sixteen years – after which he had to put in another four years as a 'veteran' (veterans did not have to perform duties within the camp, and they were only called to fight in an emergency). The pay was poor, and many of the men depended on allowances from their parents. Meals usually consisted of soup, bread, vegetables and occasionally a little wine. They seldom had any meat.

Discipline was strict. Desertion, mutiny and insubordination were punished by death. Stealing, inefficiency and lying – by flogging. The penalty for lesser offences was loss of rank.

When not campaigning, the legionaries spent their time supervising the building of roads and forts. Until the year AD 197, they were not allowed to marry – though many of them did.

Roman Britain

Celtic tribal name *ICENI*
Major Roman roads —
Routes of invasion AD 43

CALEDONA

Hadrian's Wall

HIBERNIA

BRIGANTES

Eburacum
(York)

Anglesey

Deva (Chester)

▲ Mt. Snowdon

ORDOVICES

BRITANNIA

ICENI

SILURES

Fosse Way

TRINOVANTES

CATUVELLAUNI

Camulodunum
(Colchester)

Londinium
(London)

R. Thames

R. Medway

Rutupiae
(Richborough)

REGNENSES

Isca dumnoniorum
(Exeter)

Noviomagus
(Chichester)

Romans on the March

Caesar's departure in 54 BC might have been the end of Roman military interest in Britain. For the next ninety-seven years, there was peaceful trading between the tribesmen and the merchants from Rome.

By AD 43, however, the Belgae – under King Cunobelinus whose capital was at Colchester – were carrying out raids on the French coast. Claudius, the Roman Emperor, became angry. Britain would have to be occupied. Claudius ordered his legions to march.

At about this time, Cunobelinus died. His realm was split in two. One of his sons, Togodumnus, ruled half of it; another, Caractacus, the rest.

Caesar's invasions had been journeys into the unknown. Since then, however, merchants had taken their products to settlements on the Humber, the Severn and the Trent. On their return, they were able to make useful reports about the geography of Britain, and the conditions an invading army might encounter. One encouraging fact was that the Belgic tribes were disliked by their neighbours on either side, so much that they could expect no help in battle.

The Roman army landed at Richborough in Kent. Togodumnus was killed early on in the fighting. Caractacus made a brave stand on the banks of the River Medway, but the opposition was too strong. At the day's end, he was fleeing for his life. The Roman march into Britain spread out to the four points of the compass.

West

Caractacus fled to Wales. For the next eight years, he was able to harass the Romans by making sudden attacks on their garrisons and lines of communication. Eventually, he and his family were captured, probably somewhere near Mount Snowdon. He was taken to Rome in chains, but Claudius admired his courage so much that he spared his life.

On the far side of the Menai Strait, Anglesey was in the hands of the Celtic priests, the Druids. The Romans had heard they carried out human sacrifices. It was not to be tolerated. They crossed the water in boats; the cavalry's horses swam. The engagement on the other side was brief and extremely bloody. When the fighting stopped, many of the Druids lay dead on their own altars.

South

To the west of the Roman landing place in Kent, the country was occupied by a tribe named the Regnenses. The king of the Regnenses was Cogidubnus; his capital was at Noviomagus (now Chichester). Cogidubnus did not want trouble. Indeed, he was so helpful that Claudius gave him more land; confirmed him as a king and appointed him one of his representatives in Britain. Cogidubnus did so well out of it, that he was able to build himself a magnificent palace.

East

The King of the Iceni in East Anglia was also co-operative. When he died in AD 60, his will stipulated that Nero (who had become Emperor in AD 54, when Claudius was poisoned by his wife Agrippina) should share his estate with his widow, Boadicea (Boudicca), and their children.

Boadicea dutifully sent Nero his share of the bequest but the Emperor now insisted that he must have *all* the dead man's property. A contingent of infantry was mustered at Colchester. Some while later, the men arrived at Boadicea's home near Norwich.

It was a dirty business. The palace was looted, the queen's daughters were assaulted, and she was whipped. Nero was no doubt satisfied, but he had lost the Iceni's loyalty for ever.

Gathering support from other tribes, Boadicea declared war on the Romans. But, no matter how brave they might be, her warriors were no match for the well drilled legions of Rome. After minor successes, the angry queen fought her last battle on the edge of London (somewhere near the site of King's Cross station). At the cost of 400 casualties, the Romans killed 30,000 of her men. Boadicea escaped and hurried back to Norfolk, where she took poison.

North

In AD 84, a Roman expedition marched into the Highlands of Scotland. On a hill known as Mount Graupius, in the region of Inverness, the legionaries met a force of tall men (most of whom seemed to have red hair) armed with long swords and circular shields. The Romans won, but this was far from the end of the matter.

Some years later, the 9th Legion was wiped out while marching to Tayside. Unwilling to lose any more troops, the Romans withdrew to England. In AD 121, Hadrian's Wall, (named after the reigning Emperor) was built. Seventy miles long, it stretched from the North Sea to the Solway Firth. There were small forts at one-mile intervals, ditches, castles, camps and signal towers. Apart from sending an occasional patrol out into the Lowlands, the Romans kept to the English side of it. Scotland was left alone.

In AD 367, the wall was overwhelmed by the Picts who inhabited Scotland. They came back in 383 – only to find that all the garrisons had been removed. The Romans now had other things to worry about.

While the Picts were harrying them in the north, parties of Scots (from Ireland), Saxons and Gauls from France were making raids on the English coast. But the Roman occupation was nearing its end. In 406, the legions were withdrawn from Britain. Rome itself was now under attack and they were badly needed for its defence.

Below: Hadrian's Wall was built in AD121. It ran from the North Sea to the Solway Firth.

Hadrian: the Roman emperor with a talent for building walls. This larger-than-life statue was dredged up from the Thames.

Life in Roman Britain

Rome was a city, and wherever her citizens went, they built towns. The Britons had never seen such places before, and they did not feel at home in them or take kindly to the Roman way of life.

For thousands of years, the Britons had been banded together in tribes, each with its own king. The Romans changed the system completely. They introduced one ruler for the whole of England, Scotland and Wales. There was now a central government; and laws that had to be obeyed from one end of the land to the others. These laws were administered by courts of justice, a word that Britons had never heard before. The essence of it was that a man was innocent unless he was proven guilty.

But, above all things, the Romans were builders. They constructed fine roads. They erected magnificent houses complete with plumbing. They also taught new methods of agriculture.

Unfortunately, they also demanded high taxation. For the wealthy man who lived in a villa, life was never better. For the slaves who served him, it could be very hard indeed.

Nevertheless, for the 300 years and more that the Romans ruled Britain, there was mostly peace. Trade prospered: civilization had arrived.

The Romans were more than warriors: they were civil engineers and artists, too. Among their greater accomplishments was the composition of beautiful mosaics to decorate floors and, even, pavements.

At Lullingstone in Kent, this Roman villa was once the home of a wealthy family. The walls were 2½ metres high; mosaics on the floor depicted ancient legends; and among its amenities was a bath house. The original inhabitants were pagans. Remains of a Christian chapel suggest a change of belief – probably in the 4th century AD.

The Anglo-Saxon Invasions

When Saxon kings were buried, their possessions were interred with them. At Sutton Hoo, Suffolk, a 27-metre-long ship was discovered. It was loaded with treasures – such as this helmet.

The Roman Empire was in trouble. By the middle of the 4th century, Rome itself was under attack by barbarians from the north and east. The legions had to be withdrawn from Britain. With no soldiers to defend it, the island was now at the mercy of invaders.

In 446, a British chief wrote to the Emperor. It was a sad, desperate appeal – asking him to send back the legions. He received no reply.

The Romans had been prepared to teach the Britons so much. They had shown the way to civilization, but the Britons had refused to learn. The system of central government collapsed; small local kingdoms, each with its own ruler, were established. Had they been united, they might have driven off the barbarians from across the Channel. All too often, however, they were fighting among themselves.

A few cities, such as St Albans, maintained the Roman way of life. The majority – Bath, for example – became deserted. Their streets were empty; their buildings falling into ruins.

Ireland had not been invaded by the Romans. Her people were still living in the last of the Iron Ages. Using boats made from skins, Scots (which was probably the Irish word for 'raiders') crossed the sea, and helped themselves to portions of south-west Scotland. From elsewhere in Scotland, the Picts (who had overrun the Lowlands in 209) brought havoc to the north of England. In southern and eastern England, the trouble came from Europe.

About the year 449, a king named Vortigern – whose realm stretched from Wales to Kent – became anxious. In the north, there was anarchy. It could not be long until it spread to the south-east. In an attempt to make himself more secure, he offered land on the Isle of Thanet in Kent to a pair of Jutish chiefs (from north-west Germany) named Hengist and Horsa. They accepted.

Poor Vortigern: his plans went wrong. Hengist and Horsa quickly realized that this was a land of opportunity. The Britons seemed to be a cowardly people, unable to defend the little that was theirs. Land and plunder were to be had by anyone who came and took them. They sent back messages to Europe and their fellow countrymen poured in.

Hengist slew Horsa and overwhelmed the whole of Kent. Vortigern was now even worse off; but that, as the Romans had discovered, was the snag about employing mercenary fighters. They usually ended up by taking the very thing they had been hired to defend.

And the invaders continued to arrive. The pattern was nearly always the same. At first, there were small parties; then much larger numbers. The Angles (from the Elbe and Rhine districts) and the Saxons (from north west Germany) moved in. The former occupied Norfolk and Suffolk; the latter – Essex, Middlesex, Sussex and eastern parts of Wessex.

The newcomers pushed on. Following the rivers, they made their way into a land of forests, rough moorland, and bogs. Occasionally, they came across the mouldering remains of a Roman city. They had never seen buildings on this scale, and they assumed they had been built by a race of giants. They didn't care for them. Instead of occupying them, they built their settlements beyond the defensive walls.

On and on they moved – through forests inhabited only by wolves and bears, clearing away the trees and making farms. They were tough, brutal men who knew no mercy. It is impossible not to admire their courage; but, for the Britons, their arrival was catastrophic. Those who remained behind became slaves. The majority sought sanctuary amid the hills of Wales or Scotland. Nowhere else was safe.

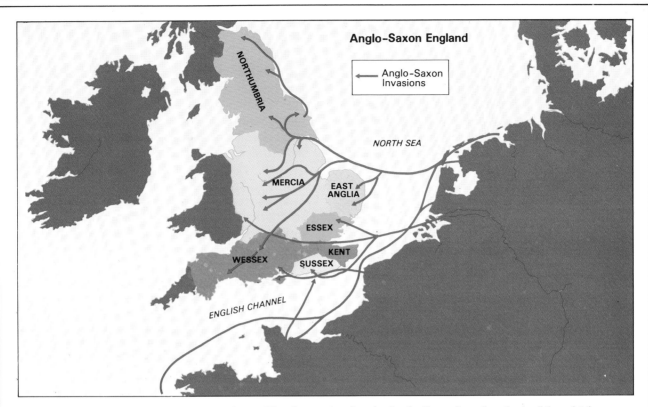

Above: A map of England divided into the Seven Kingdoms, showing the Anglo-Saxon invasions in the 5th and 6th centuries. Below: A scene in the Bayeaux Tapestry depicts Edward the Confessor talking to Harold of Wessex. Was Harold Edward's rightful heir? William of Normandy thought not.

King Arthur

The popular picture of King Arthur and his knights is of a band of chivalrous gentlemen clad in shining armour. This is far from the truth. So far as we know, Arthur was a general serving a British king named Ambrosius Aurchanus. When the monarch died, he took over the task of harassing the Saxons. His troops were probably mounted, and disciplined like Roman soldiers. Many of the engagements seem to have been fought at crossroads and fords. Possibly, they were ambushes.

Arthur's men certainly seem to have been unusually mobile – making sudden attacks, and then melting away into the forest. In the year 516, they fought a full scale battle against the Saxons at a place named Mount Badon somewhere in the West Country. They were victorious, and this success seems to have halted the Saxon advance for the better part of fifty years.

King Arthur was killed in a civil war – about twenty years afterwards.

The Seven Kingdoms

It took one hundred years for the Anglo-Saxons to complete their occupation. Britain now was divided up into seven kingdoms. Among them were Northumbria, which reached from the Humber to Edinburgh and eventually westwards to the Lancashire coast; Mercia – the Midlands; and Wessex – southern England. Offa, the ruler of Mercia (he who built Offa's Dyke running from Prestatyn to the Wye as a boundary between England and Wales) once described himself as 'King of the English', but this was a mere boast. When, in the 9th century, King Egbert of Wessex helped himself to Kent and other Saxon lands in the south-east, it became generally accepted that the Wessex king was the senior monarch – and that, therefore, he ruled England.

Although these early kings were based in strategically sited towns, they spent much of their time travelling – collecting rents and taxes and administering justice. The Saxons believed in handing down the throne from father to son – unless the heir turned out to be unsuitable. In such cases an advisory council appointed another member of the royal family.

Apart from supervising the law and collecting his money, the king settled feuds, led hunting and military expeditions, and gave sumptuous banquets. He was assisted by an official known as the Ealdorman.

The Anglo-Saxon kings did not maintain large standing armies. They did, however, keep small, well-equipped, bands of warriors for emergencies. In wartime, these forces were strengthened by peasants conscripted from the fields. They fought with fanaticism; for they knew that, if they were captured, they and their families would probably spend the rest of their lives in slavery.

The small farmer depended for his land, his livestock and his supplies, on his local lord. In return for these things, he spent two or three days each week working for his master. Sometimes – after, for example, an exceptionally bad harvest – the only chance of survival was for the whole family to become slaves. The alternative was to go without food. It was a dismal outlook. As they knew very well, even the law against murder did not apply to these unfortunate people. If a slave was slain, his killer could be prosecuted only for 'destruction of property'.

Tintagel Castle in Cornwall was built in 1145 by a son of Henry I. Before that, this site had been occupied by a monastery. It is one of several sites in Britain that has been connected with the legend of King Arthur.

The Lindisfarne Gospels were copied out by hand at the end of the 7th century. The task took the monks 23 years. The bishop supplied the decorations.

Christianity Comes to Britain

The Romans had brought their own religious customs with them to Britain, and built temples in which to worship their gods. Apart from their loathing of the Druids, they were tolerant of the islanders' beliefs. As in so many other things, the men of Rome and the people of Britain went their own, different, ways.

But one morning in 313 an event occurred that was to affect the whole world, and which, eventually, enabled Romans and Britons to worship side-by-side. The Roman Emperor Constantine I was converted to Christianity.

Inevitably, word of this reached the empire's outposts; and, just as certainly, the old gods were put on one side. The message of Christianity was universal. The Britons, too, accepted it.

But when the Romans withdrew, the Barbarians brought their pagan gods with them. For 150 years, Christianity was driven underground. When it returned, the message travelled across the land from the north and from the south.

During one of their raids on Wales, the Irish had snatched a Christian boy named Patrick from his home near the River Severn. Patrick was sold as a slave. He learned the Irish language; and, some years later, he escaped to England. He studied to become a priest. In 432, the Pope ordered him back to Ireland as a missionary. Within ten years, Patrick had converted very nearly the whole island.

Thanks to his work, it was an Irishman who

Conflict

The coming of Christianity to Britain was a kind of pincer movement. The Celtic priests from the north taught a more tolerant faith than the missionaries from Rome. They did not believe in the Pope's divine authority – they even celebrated Easter on a different day. They were monks who roamed from place to place, whilst the followers of Augustine built churches and established bishops. Because a bishop's sphere of influence was so large, it had to be divided up into parishes, with a priest in charge of each.

In 663, the Celtic clergy and the Roman priests met at Whitby in an attempt to reconcile their views. The main object was to agree about the date of Easter. At the end of the discussions, the Roman opinion was accepted about this and several other matters. The Celtic priests retired quietly to their monasteries.

King Cnut was a man of great power – and of wisdom, too. He believed in good relations with the church (a change from his unruly ancestors). Here, he is seen giving an altar cross to a recently built abbey near Winchester.

took Christianity to Scotland. In 563, a monk named Columba landed on the island of Iona off the western coast. He built a monastery, and taught the gospel to the Picts. From this base, the new faith spread across Scotland and southwards into England. Seventy years later, monks from Iona were preaching in Northumberland, where they built a monastery at Lindisfarne.

Christianity returned to southern England in 597, when Pope Gregory sent forty monks, led by a man named Augustine, from Rome. These men were afraid. They had heard such tales of British brutality that, before they had travelled very far, they asked Augustine to return and beg Gregory to release them from their task. But Gregory refused and the journey continued.

They were fortunate. They landed on Thanet. As it happened, the ruler of Kent, King Ethelbert, had a Christian wife. He told them to go ahead with their work; and even offered them lodgings in his capital at Canterbury. Some while later, he himself became converted.

During the first year of their mission, Augustine and his monks baptised ten thousand people.

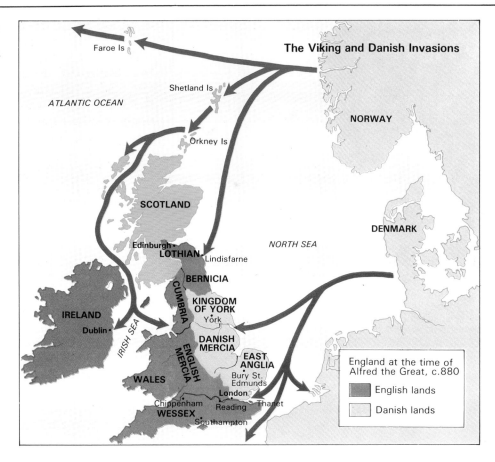

Right: England in the reign of King Alfred was a land divided between the Danes and the men of Wessex. King Alfred could never rest easy. He built a navy and fortified his towns against the day when war would come. The arrows show the Danish and Viking invasion routes in the 8th and 9th centuries.

The Viking and Danish Invasions

ATLANTIC OCEAN

Faroe Is

Shetland Is

NORWAY

Orkney Is

SCOTLAND

NORTH SEA

DENMARK

Edinburgh
LOTHIAN
Lindisfarne

BERNICIA

CUMBRIA
KINGDOM
OF YORK
York

IRELAND
Dublin

IRISH SEA

DANISH
MERCIA

ENGLISH
MERCIA

EAST
ANGLIA

WALES
Bury St.
Edmunds
London
Chippenham
Reading
Thanet
WESSEX
Southampton

England at the time of
Alfred the Great, c.880

■ English lands
□ Danish lands

Left: The prow of an excavated Viking ship. It somehow expresses the vessel's qualities of strength, sea-worthiness, and speed.

Warriors from the North

They came from the cold, harsh lands of the north, like creatures of prey. Their own countries had little to offer them. To prosper, they had to travel; to be utterly ruthless, to kill and to rob without the smallest twinge of conscience.

They were the Norsemen; the most magnificent seamen the world has ever known. They crossed the Atlantic; explored the Arctic fringe into Russia; made voyages to the Mediterranean; and paid many visits to the British Isles.

In the early part of 793, there were disturbing omens in England. The roof of St Peter's church in York appeared to drip with blood. There were exceptionally high winds, and the sky was rent by lightning. Some people said that they saw fiery dragons in the heavens. Afterwards, there was a famine.

That June, the meaning of these portents became clear. The longships of the Vikings (each with a dragon on its prow) came to Lindisfarne. The monastery was sacked. Many of the monks were drowned or clubbed to death – the rest were taken away as slaves. All the treasures were removed.

As the years went by, the raids became more numerous. The Norsemen occupied the Shetland Islands, the Orkneys and the Faroes. From these bases, they plundered the west coast of Scotland and southwards as far as the River Mersey. They attacked Ireland, whilst, on the east coast of England, the Danes harried Norfolk and Suffolk.

Whenever the Norsemen came, their attacks followed the same pattern. As soon as they were ashore, they rounded up every horse in the vicinity. Then they rode inland, looting, burning, killing. Presently, rich with booty, they returned to their ships and sailed away.

But these operations were the work of small chieftains whose only interest was in the plunder. When, in 851, the Danes came to the isles of Thanet and Sheppey in Kent, it was quite another matter. They remained there throughout the winter. And it was obvious that they were now considering a full scale invasion.

One day in 839, twelve years before the Danes' winter holiday in Kent, a Norwegian named Turgeis had landed in Ireland and founded the city of Dublin. He proclaimed himself 'King of all the foreigners'. Turgeis was something of a missionary. His ambition was to convert the island's population from Christianity to his own pagan beliefs. The natives were not impressed. They drowned him in a lake.

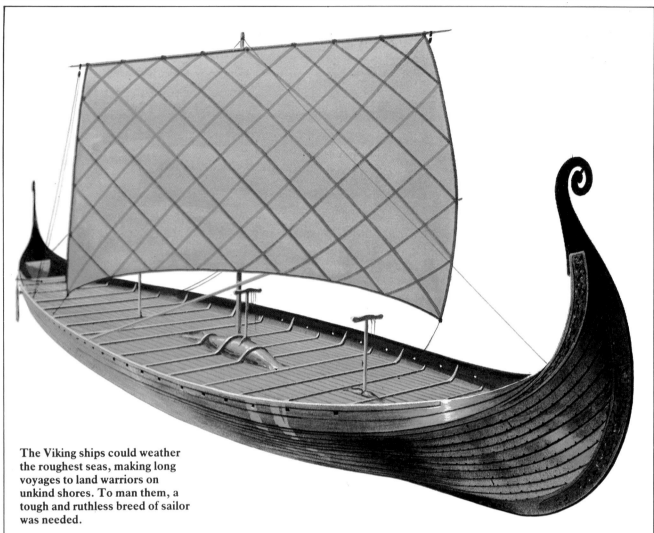

The Viking ships could weather the roughest seas, making long voyages to land warriors on unkind shores. To man them, a tough and ruthless breed of sailor was needed.

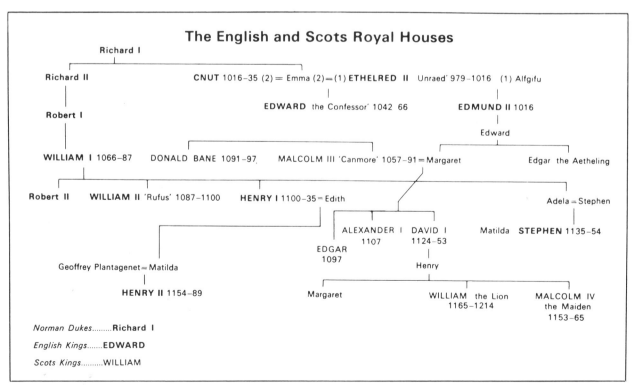

The English and Scots Royal Houses

Richard I

Richard II   **CNUT** 1016–35 (2) = Emma (2)=(1) **ETHELRED II** Unraed' 979–1016 (1) Alfgifu

      EDWARD the Confessor' 1042 66   **EDMUND II** 1016

Robert I

      Edward

WILLIAM I 1066–87   DONALD BANE 1091–97   MALCOLM III 'Canmore' 1057–91 = Margaret   Edgar the Aetheling

Robert II   **WILLIAM II** 'Rufus' 1087–1100   **HENRY I** 1100–35 = Edith   Adela = Stephen

      ALEXANDER I   DAVID I   Matilda   **STEPHEN** 1135–54
      1107   1124–53

     EDGAR
     1097

Geoffrey Plantagenet = Matilda   Henry

   HENRY II 1154–89   Margaret   WILLIAM the Lion   MALCOLM IV
      1165–1214   the Maiden
      1153–65

Norman Dukes.........**Richard I**

English Kings.......**EDWARD**

Scots Kings..........WILLIAM

In Scotland, the Vikings, the Picts and the Scots were all at war with one another. At last, in the same year as Turgeis founded Dublin, there was a decisive battle. After the fighting had stopped, a Scot named Kenneth was able to proclaim himself first King of Scotland.

Down in England, the country was ripe for invasion. In 866, York fell. The kingdom of Mercia followed, and then it was East Anglia's turn. By the winter of 878, only Wessex remained independent.

The Danes had established a base at Reading, and their supplies were coming up the Thames. At first it seemed as if Wessex might share the fate of the other kingdoms. In the winter of 878, the 22-year old King Alfred was forced to flee and hide up among the Somerset marshes. But Alfred returned in the spring. He gathered an army, and routed the Danish forces at a battle near Southampton. Two days later, at Chippenham, the Danish leader – Guthrum – surrendered.

Guthrum was given a lesson in Christian kindness. Far from putting him to death, Alfred offered him generous terms. The Danes, he said, must promise to quit Wessex, but they could have a large slice of eastern England. They were not to strip it bare with another orgy of plunder, but to settle down and farm it. Guthrum agreed.

He must have found this demonstration of charity convincing. Not long afterwards, he asked to be baptised, and he named Alfred as his godfather.

Betrayal
King Edmund of East Anglia was defeated by the Danes near Thetford in Norfolk. The story goes that, fleeing from the enemy, he hid under a bridge. A young bride on her way to her wedding noticed his gold spurs glistening in the sun. She betrayed him. Edmund was captured, and was offered his life in return for accepting Danish sovereignty and Danish gods. He refused and was put to death. The town of Bury St Edmunds in Suffolk is named after him.

Danelaw

The lands given to or taken by the Danes were known as Danelaw, just as the money spent in attempts to buy them off was known as Danegold.

For the next few years, peace settled on England. The Danes tilled their new soil. Alfred went about his business, much of it concerned with precautions against another attack. He built a chain of fortified boroughs and (something that England had never had before) a fleet. Since his fellow countrymen had no experience of naval warfare, he hired his mariners from the Low Countries.

Alfred's son, Edward the Elder, merged Wessex with Mercia and continued to keep the Danes in their place. His heir, Athelstan proudly called himself 'the King of the English and all the nations round about'. Three of his sisters were, admittedly, married to important rulers. Nevertheless, it was an exaggeration.

In 979, Alfred's great great grandson, King Edward (known as 'the Martyr'), went to see his half-brother, Ethelred, at Corfe Castle in Dorset. Exactly what happened is a mystery. Edward was certainly murdered, but who killed him? Some say it was Ethelred, but he was only eleven years old at the time. His mother seems a more likely villain, for, once Edward was dead, she quickly proclaimed her son king.

Ethelred went from one blunder to another. His greatest folly was a massacre of all the Danes in Wessex. The victims included the King of Norway's daughter. Afterwards, Ethelred had to flee for his life to France. A Dane named Cnut took over the crown and ruled until 1035.

The unhappy King Ethelred died in 1016. His son and heir, Edward, spent the next twenty-two years in exile. For much of the time, he stayed with a distant relative named William, Duke of Normandy.

Known as 'the Confessor', Edward was a very religious man. He was, perhaps, more suited to be a priest or a scholar than a king. But in 1042, a deputation of Saxon nobles came to him and asked him to rule England, and he agreed.

He was ill at ease at the high-spirited Saxon Court, preferring to spend his time overseeing the construction of an abbey at Westminster. It was completed in 1065, but Edward was too ill to attend the first service. He died a week afterwards. Towards the end of his reign, the future King Harold (son of Earl Godwin of Wessex) attended to most affairs of state.

The Unready
King Ethelred is usually known as 'Ethelred the Unready'. The actual word was 'unrede', which meant 'ill-advised'. However, either description is appropriate, for Ethelred was seldom ready and nearly always ill-advised.

The World of Saxon England

Despite all the intrigues and killings at Court, life in the Saxon countryside went on quietly and industriously. A village was still composed of small huts – each about six metres long – with the floors sunk beneath the ground. Heavy ploughs drawn by teams of oxen were used for turning over the soil: for harvesting, scythes were employed.

The towns were centres for defence, administration and trading. Each was protected by a fortified wall. In times of trouble, the country people took shelter there. No village was more than twenty miles from one of these sanctuaries.

When the Romans departed, they left behind a magnificent network of roads. Their main purpose had been the movement of armies over long distances. The Saxons used them as links between one market town and another. They did not, however, keep them in good repair.

Carts with two or four wheels were used for short journeys; large wagons, with leather roofs, for longer trips. But, whenever possible, the Saxons preferred to use the rivers for transport.

Clothes

The men in the days of King Harold wore trousers or stockings with cross-garters; short tunics, and cloaks that were fastened at the shoulders by brooches. The dresses of the women were of wool – or silk if the lady was wealthy. They wore beautifully crafted brooches and necklaces. The higher the social rank of the wearer, the brighter were the colours used in his or her costume.

Cash

The Romans had introduced coins to Britain. The Anglo-Saxons did not mint any money until the 7th century. At first, gold was used – later, silver coins were made. The production of coins was the king's concern, though the Archbishops of Canterbury and York were allowed to manufacture their own. Many towns had small mints.

Crime

Ethelbert of Kent was responsible for ordering the law to be written down in English for the first time. Many crimes were tried by ordeals supervised by the clergy. For example, an accused man was thrown into cold water. If he floated, it was believed to be a sign from God that he was guilty. Or he was made to remove a stone from a pot of boiling water. His injury was bandaged, and if it healed within three days, he was acquitted.

Crimes in which the culprit was caught in the act were more heavily punished than those in which his guilt was shown by an ordeal. Arson, murder, treachery to one's lord, and some thefts were punished by death (often hanging). Mutilation and banishment into slavery were lesser penalties. The most common of all were fines. Whatever the offence, the person responsible had to compensate his victim. If a man stole from the church, he had to pay twelve times the value of his theft – from the king, nine times the value.

Art

The Anglo-Saxons were tough and sometimes brutal. Nevertheless, they were by no means barbarians. Among them were some fine artists who could turn their hands to religious paintings, the design of churches and the production of beautiful ornaments. Indeed, the short reign of Harold and the longer rule of Edward the Confes-

Left: Anglo-Saxon men – who were tough and often brutal – dressed comfortably. Those who wore stockings decorated them with cross-garters.

Right: Windows in Deerhurst Church, Gloucestershire, (it was built in 1056) survive as a tribute to Saxon artistry.

sor marked an important period in the history of English art.

Court Life

Life at court depended on the king. If, during the reign of Cnut, somebody sat in the wrong seat at the royal table, he was sent to the far end. The others then pelted him with greasy bones. He was not allowed to throw them back.

Visitors to the court from Wales seem to have been an unruly lot. They had to be cautioned not to strike the queen – nor to snatch things from her. Edward the Confessor's wife spent much of her time embroidering robes for her husband, and giving grammar lessons to students (for which she was paid). Her husband used to keep the royal funds in a box hidden in his bedroom.

The Alfred Jewel was discovered near an island in Somerset in 1693. Created from gold and crystal, it shows a man holding two sceptres and is inscribed with the words 'Alfred ordered me to be made'. Its date: probably AD 871 – the year Alfred became King of Wessex.

The Norman Conquest

When Edward the Confessor died in 1066, William, Duke of Normandy, asserted that he had been promised the throne of England. He also said that Harold, who had visited Normandy in 1058, had pledged himself to support this claim.

Harold did nothing of the kind. Forgetting whatever promises he may have made, he helped himself to the throne. From that moment, a Norman invasion became extremely likely, and Harold knew it.

The two men at the heart of this drama were very different. William was the illegitimate son of Robert, Duke of Normandy, known as 'Robert the Devil'. Aged thirty-eight, he was six years younger than Harold; a tallish man with thinning black hair and twirling moustaches. His attitude to warfare was original by the standards of those days. Instead of relying on brute force, he introduced carefully thought out tactics.

He used his archers rather like artillery: to soften up the defences and cut holes in the enemy ranks before launching an assault. As for his horse soldiers, he employed them in much the manner of present day tanks.

King Harold was forty-four when he took over the throne. He was a thick-set, stocky individual with great stamina and courage. Although he thought himself a cunning fighter – a general who might spring a few surprises on his enemy – his ability was not really to be compared with William's.

Throughout the summer of 1066, Harold watched and waited for William's invasion fleet. He occupied a headquarters on the Isle of Wight; his ships patrolled the Channel. But the Normans did not come. By the end of August, the sailors were running short of food, and the vessels were in a sorry state. Harold ordered them to London to be refitted.

In Normandy, William must have smiled with satisfaction. The way across the sea was now clear. With his warships in dock, there was nothing Harold could do to harass the invasion fleet.

Had he known about it, he would have been even more pleased. This vengeful Norman duke was not the only Continental ruler with his eye on England. Harald Hardrada, King of Norway, had similar ideas. In late August, much to Harold's dismay, he suddenly launched his own invasion by landing an army at the mouth of the Humber.

Harold hurried north to meet him. On 20

The Bayeaux Tapestry tells the story of the Battle of Hastings in much the manner of a huge strip cartoon. Seventy metres long, it shows 72 scenes. This one depicts the death of Harold. He was not killed by an arrow in the eye, but cut down by Norman knights.

September, he defeated the Norwegian forces at the Battle of Stamford Bridge. Harald Hardrada was killed in action.

Two days later, William's men landed at Pevensey in Sussex without any opposition. They spent the next few days ravaging the countryside – killing, burning, and looting – while, fresh from one battle, Harold and his soldiers marched south to fight another.

By early morning on 14 October, the two sides were in position for what was to become known as the Battle of Hastings. Harold's troops had occupied the crest of a hill at the edge of the forest – seven miles from the Norman landing place. There were about eleven thousand of them, armed with clubs, axes and short iron swords.

The Norman army, which was now on the far side of a valley, amounted to eight thousand. But these men were more professional than Harold's. Nor were they weary after two forced marches with a battle against the Norwegians in between.

At ten o'clock that morning, William nodded to a trumpeter, who sounded the advance. The English were massed in eight ranks protected by a wall of shields. Whatever victory might be in store for the Normans was obviously going to be

hard won.

The Norman infantry moved forward while, over their heads, the archers' arrows covered their advance. Immediately gaps began to appear in Harold's ranks. Then, suddenly, the barrage from the bowmen ceased. The infantry moved in and the real carnage began.

Harold's soldiers may have been tired after the events of the past week or so, but accounts of the Normans' behaviour in Sussex had made them angry. They fought with desperate ferocity and courage. Nevertheless, William's foot soldiers managed to hack holes in the English ranks – holes that made it possible for the cavalry to charge through, wheel round and attack from the rear.

But the battle was far from over. Quite early, the troops on the Norman left flank wavered. Then, with heavy casualties, they retreated towards the safety of the valley. Some of Harold's men immediately broke ranks and pursued them. It was a fatal mistake.

Cut off from the rest of the English army, it was an easy job for William's horsemen to gallop up and cut them to pieces. And it gave William an idea, which he used later in the day.

Things were still fairly evenly matched. To improve his situation, William ordered his right flank to advance – and then *pretend* to retreat. The English, forgetful of the previous disaster, swallowed the bait. Once they were in the open, the cavalry slaughtered them.

Harold's army had now lost both its flanks. The survivors were clustered around the command post. In spite of heavy losses, they were fighting as furiously as ever.

William now had another inspiration. He ordered his archers to aim their shots higher. This meant that the arrows would inflict casualties on the rear ranks. It worked with horrible efficiency.

The end came at about five o'clock. Twenty Norman knights charged the English position, trying desperately to force their way through it. Only four survived, but that was sufficient. They found King Harold and killed him with their swords. (Harold was *not* slain by an arrow in one of his eyes. The story, though popular, has no truth in it.)

With their leader dead, the fight went out of the English. Those who could manage it, quietly withdrew into the deep forest leaving behind their wounded. The battle was over. The reign of William the Conqueror had begun.

The Middle Ages

*War, plague, treachery, murder, and
rebellion were the dark side of the Middle Ages.
But there were innovations, too. For the baron,
there was a castle in which his warriors assembled
in times of violence; for the priest, a monastery.
Some people enjoyed wealth and honour but the
vast majority suffered poverty.*

Corfe Castle, Dorset.

A Plan for Britain

On Christmas Day 1066, Duke William of Normandy was crowned King of England in Westminster Abbey. A few hours of bitter fighting near Hastings had given him a new kingdom. They had not, however, rewarded him with the devotion and obedience of his new subjects. The Saxons had been overpowered and they were angry. Given the smallest opportunity, they would rise up and attempt to win back the land.

For his part, William was not content with England alone. There was Scotland to the north and Wales to the west. He wanted them as well.

To govern his new realm, William allotted large estates to the two hundred barons who had come with him from Normandy. But he was crafty. To prevent them from banding together against him, he scattered their estates all over the country. Nor did he *give* them land. He leased it to them in return for certain services. They had to raise troops when he needed them. They had to come to court whenever he bade them. If he had a problem, they had to advise him.

This was the so-called feudal system. Each baron ruled his little empire (or *manor* as it was called). He kept as much of the land as he needed for himself, and distributed the rest to his knights. In return, they recruited the men and arms to meet the king's requirements.

The knights broke up their slices of land into even smaller units, which they leased to serfs. In return for scraps of soil, these men had to supply their masters with free labour; to serve as soldiers when ordered; to pledge their loyalty and obedience.

A serf could not even marry his daughter to a man in another manor without first getting his master's permission.

Life for the knights and barons was good in Norman England. For others, especially the Saxons, it was atrocious. Suppose, for example, a Norman was murdered. If the killer was not caught, the citizens of the town where the crime occurred were fined. But if the victim turned out to be a Saxon, no penalty was demanded.

The Saxons were taxed, tormented and treated as second class citizens. Inevitably, there were minor rebellions – and, just as inevitably, they were brutally put down.

But Scotland and Wales had yet to be conquered. In 1072, William marched his armies north on a brilliant campaign. When they reached the river Tay, they found ships of the fleet waiting for them. Malcolm, the Scottish king, surrendered. He declared himself William's man. He even handed over his eldest son, Duncan, as hostage.

Seven years later, Malcolm seems to have forgotten his promise. He marched his troops south – burning and pillaging – and reached the Tyne before being turned back. In 1093, on another expedition into England, he was killed. His Queen died of a broken heart. Duncan, the son who had been surrendered all those years ago, was allowed to return to Scotland as king. In view of his father's conduct, Duncan was lucky to be alive.

The invasion of Wales was more gradual. The Norman earls and their forces advanced slowly up the Wye valley, and from bases at Shrewsbury and Chester. Gradually, bit by bit, they nibbled away – until the Welsh were driven into the hills.

As in England, the Normans built castles wherever they went. Towns such as Cardiff, Swansea and Newport grew from communities at the foot of the castle walls.

One of the last Saxons to hold out against William was Hereward the Wake – so named from his connection with the Wake family in Lincolnshire. He operated in the vicinity of the Isle of Ely, where the marshes made it difficult for the Normans to manoeuvre large forces. Sometimes, he took shelter in the island's monastery.

During one foray, when his men were sur-

The pecking order of the Feudal System had the king at the top and the peasants so far beneath him they were almost out of sight. In between came barons, priests and knights.

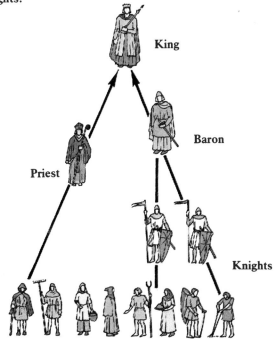

King

Baron

Priest

Knights

Peasants

rounded, Hereward escaped. Later, however, he was captured. But by this time, William had become so impressed by his courage, that he granted him a pardon.

By the time William died in 1087, the conquest was complete. The only part of the British Isles that had not submitted to the Normans was Ireland. Wisely, no doubt, the Conqueror never tried to send troops across the Irish Sea.

All the land belonged to William I. It was estimated that he kept one-quarter of it for his own use; leased two-fifths of it to the barons; and gave the remainder to the Church. In spite of his ruthlessness, William was a devout Christian. He provided large sums for the building of churches and cathedrals. His bishops had considerable power – acting, in many ways, like barons.

None the less, in church matters, as in everything else, he was in complete control. No bishop was allowed to visit Rome without his permission, nor, indeed, to write to the Pope. If the Pope sent any instructions to his clergy in England, they could not be carried out without William's permission.

Concerning the lands he kept for his own use, William took a particular interest in the forests. They were admirable for hunting, and the New Forest in Hampshire was declared a royal game reserve. Everything within it belonged to the king. It was as much an offence to gather wood for the fire as it was to poach deer. The penalty for either might be the chopping off of a hand.

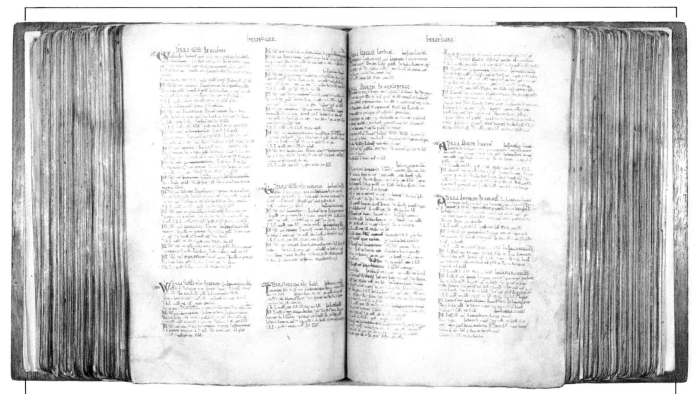

The Domesday Book

The Domesday Book: a useful list of England's assets.

Twenty years after he had conquered England, William decided he needed a complete list of his possessions on this side of the Channel. It was to be a detailed account of the royal estates and those of his tenants-in-chief. Since nearly all the country was involved, the result was rather like a present day census, though much more elaborate. It included facts about the population, the divisions of land, the houses, and so on. But William wanted to see what changes had occurred during his reign. Consequently, the investigators had to find out about the past as well as the present.

The result of this very complicated work was called the 'Domesday Book'. All the evidence was given on oath; all the information was checked to make sure it was accurate. The questioning was so thorough, that somebody said it was like Judgement Day (or Doomsday; it used to be spelt Domesday).

Among the uses of the Domesday Book were those of suggesting opportunities of raising more taxes, and of estimating the country's military strength. The latter was important. William was continually worried about the possibility of an invasion by the Danes.

Law and Order

William I was succeeded by his red-haired son, William Rufus. He levied high taxes from the barons; helped himself to money that belonged to the monasteries. Nobody liked him; most people hated him; and everybody was delighted when he was killed in 1100 while hunting in the New Forest. His death was supposed to be the result of an arrow accidentally let off in his direction by Sir Walter Tyrell. But was it really a mistake? There were many who believed that Sir Walter had done England an excellent service.

William Rufus was succeeded by his younger brother, Henry I (1100–35). Henry had only one legitimate son, and he was drowned in the Channel. Consequently, his daughter, Matilda, became his heir.

England had never been ruled by a queen, and the barons were not too keen on the idea. They invited her cousin, Stephen, to take over the throne. But Matilda, not unreasonably, objected.

While Stephen and she fought for the crown, centralized government – the safeguard of law and order – came close to breaking down. The barons, especially, exploited the lack of royal supervision. They plundered their peasants' lands; violently settled personal feuds; and built more castles.

By the time of Stephen's death, the country needed a strong and wise ruler to pull it together. Fortunately Matilda's son Henry II – who succeeded Stephen in 1154 – was just the man.

Henry had already inherited the French provinces of Anjou, Normandy and Maine from his father. Later, he married the divorced wife of the French king, Eleanor, who presented him with the duchy of Aquitaine. These possessions on the Continent became known as the Angevin Empire. But Henry is better known as the first Plantagenet king – after *Planta Genista*, the Latin name for the sprig of bloom he made his emblem.

The new monarch was short, sturdy, and inclined to put on weight. When he flew into a rage, which was often, his eyes became bloodshot. But he was extremely intelligent and had enormous energy. Even when he was in church, he wrote and dictated. Life at court became spartan. As for the courtiers, those less energetic than the king were almost perpetually tired.

But Henry brought back law and order to England. He introduced a system of travelling judges. He detested the 'ordeal' method of determining guilt, and empowered juries to give ver-

Above: Queen Matilda and King Stephen. Matilda claimed the crown was hers; Stephen knew it was his.

The Angevin Empire c.1175

Edinburgh

IRISH SEA

York

Dublin

NORTH SEA

Bristol · London

FLANDERS

ENGLISH CHANNEL

CHAMPAGNE

DUCHY OF NORMANDY · Paris

DUCHY OF BRITTANY

MAINE

BLOIS

ANJOU Tours

TOURAINE

BURGUNDY

DUCHY OF AQUITAINE

BAY OF BISCAY

· Bordeaux

GASCONY

TOULOUSE

Lands inherited by Henry II through his mother

Lands inherited by Henry II through his father

Lands acquired after 1170

Lands acquired by Henry II through mariage to Eleanor of Aquitaine (1152)

The Kingdom of France

dicts in criminal cases. He disliked the death penalty; even a murderer was punished either by the loss of a hand, or else by imprisonment and a fine.

Since he was always on the move, government departments were established to manage his affairs. The most important was the Exchequer. It was set up in the city of Westminster – which, therefore, became the capital.

Henry's chief adviser was a man named Thomas Becket. He made Becket Chancellor and gave him great wealth and power. In 1162, he appointed him Archbishop of Canterbury. The church had always had its own courts for the trial of offending clergymen. Henry thought they were being too lenient: he expected Becket to control them. But Becket refused. The King and the Archbishop quarrelled. Henry became even more angry when, one day just before Christmas, 1170, he heard that Becket had dismissed some English Bishops. In a fit of rage, he exclaimed, 'Will no one rid me of this turbulent priest?'

On The Move
The court had to be wherever the king was. Its members helped the sovereign to settle disputes and to form policies. Since Henry II was continually on the move – in one month, he travelled 800 miles including crossing the Channel – this collection of bishops, barons and servants had to do likewise. They seldom sat down. Henry even used to take many of his meals standing up. When they lay down for a good night's sleep, they were frequently awakened at dawn to continue the journey. And when, anticipating this, they got up early, they were apt to find that the king had decided to sleep late. The people loved Henry II; his courtiers found him extremely difficult.

Four knights slipped away to do what they imagined to be their sovereign's bidding. Henry tried to recall them, but it was too late. They murdered Becket on the altar steps at Canterbury.

Three years later, Becket was made a saint. In 1174, Henry – still feeling a deep sense of guilt – ordered the monks to flog him as he walked through the streets of Canterbury.

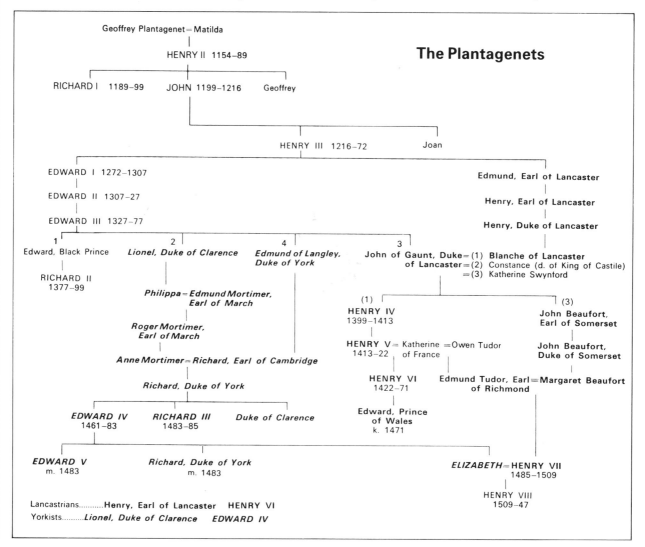

The Plantagenets

Geoffrey Plantagenet = Matilda

HENRY II 1154–89

RICHARD I 1189–99 JOHN 1199–1216 Geoffrey

HENRY III 1216–72 Joan

EDWARD I 1272–1307 Edmund, Earl of Lancaster

EDWARD II 1307–27 Henry, Earl of Lancaster

EDWARD III 1327–77 Henry, Duke of Lancaster

1 Edward, Black Prince 2 Lionel, Duke of Clarence 4 Edmund of Langley, Duke of York 3 John of Gaunt, Duke = (1) Blanche of Lancaster
of Lancaster = (2) Constance (d. of King of Castile)
= (3) Katherine Swynford

RICHARD II 1377–99

Philippa = Edmund Mortimer, Earl of March

(1) HENRY IV 1399–1413

(3) John Beaufort, Earl of Somerset

Roger Mortimer, Earl of March

HENRY V 1413–22 = Katherine of France = Owen Tudor

John Beaufort, Duke of Somerset

Anne Mortimer = Richard, Earl of Cambridge

HENRY VI 1422–71

Edmund Tudor, Earl = Margaret Beaufort of Richmond

Richard, Duke of York

EDWARD IV 1461–83 RICHARD III 1483–85 Duke of Clarence

Edward, Prince of Wales k. 1471

EDWARD V m. 1483 Richard, Duke of York m. 1483

ELIZABETH = HENRY VII 1485–1509

HENRY VIII 1509–47

Lancastrians...........Henry, Earl of Lancaster HENRY VI
Yorkists.........Lionel, Duke of Clarence EDWARD IV

A King and the Crusades

In 1095, pilgrims returning from the Holy Land had brought back alarming tales. Palestine had been overrun by the Turks. It was impossible to reach Jerusalem, and the Moslem invaders were carrying out fearful cruelties. The Pope in Rome asked the European kings to mount a crusade. Spurred on by a French monk named Peter the Hermit, the armies set off for the eastern Mediterranean. In 1099, after fierce fighting, they won back Jerusalem, which was turned into an independent Christian city-state. The pilgrims could return in safety.

Nearly a century went by. In 1187, the Sultan of Egypt – a firebrand named Saladin – marched on the Holy City with his Saracens and retook it. Again, the Pope appealed for a crusade. Among those who agreed to take part was Henry II's son, King Richard I – otherwise known as Richard Coeur de Lion (Richard the Lion Heart) for his courage in battle.

This was just the kind of thing Richard enjoyed. He had little interest in the responsibilities of government. He preferred to spend his time jousting in tournaments, or else fighting on the field of battle. He had come to the throne on Henry's death in 1189. During his reign of ten years, he spent only a few months in England.

In 1190, Richard I set out for Palestine. On the way, he captured Cyprus. In the following year, he joined up with the French and Austrian forces, and laid siege to the port of Acre. The garrison surrendered. The next target should have been Jerusalem.

But after the fall of Acre, the Crusaders quarrelled. Richard insulted Duke Leopold of Austria, and then almost came to blows with the French King, Philip Augustus. Leopold and Philip returned in a huff to Europe. Richard was now on his own.

His troops marched through rain and mud to the Holy City. When they arrived, they found that Saladin had strengthened the fortifications and reinforced his army. A siege like that at Acre would have been useless. But even though there was little threat, Saladin agreed to have talks with Richard. As it happened, the two men got on very well together. Saladin agreed that pilgrims might have safe conduct to the Holy City – though he refused to give it up.

In 1192, Richard began his long journey back to England. On the way, he was captured by the now hostile Duke Leopold. Leopold shut him up in the castle at Durnstein in Austria and demanded a ransom of £100,000.

Before departing for the crusade, Richard had put his brother John in charge of Ireland and six English counties. Instead of trying to raise the money for the king's ransom, John offered to give land to the King of France. In return, the French sovereign should agree to John's taking over the English throne. The deal misfired. The money was found, and Richard was set free.

But even after this adventure, Richard was not content to stay in England for long. There was always somebody to be fought – this time, the King of France. Like his father, Henry II, Richard was always on the move. He was killed by a well-aimed arrow while besieging the castle at the French town of Chalus in 1199.

When there was a war to be fought, Richard I did not tarry: he went off and fought it. His greatest victory was at Acre during the Crusades. The town had been under siege for two years before Richard's arrival in 1191. It fell within four weeks – its defenders crushed by his vigorous assaults.

The Barons' Revolt

After Richard I's death in action, his brother John inherited the throne. During Richard's reign, the barons had been heavily taxed to pay for the crusades. Those who hoped that John's demands would be more moderate were disappointed. This time, the money was needed to pay for another war with France.

If John's military expeditions had been successful, there might have been fewer complaints. They were not. As he bungled one campaign after another, the French won back all the royal possessions in France. The Angevin Empire over which Henry II had ruled was now gone. The barons' money was quite clearly being wasted. And John's blunders continued. He quarrelled with the Pope. English church-goers were refused the right to take communion. The king was excommunicated.

Young Prince Arthur of Brittany – John's nephew – had been recognized by Richard I as his heir. But Richard had been too busy to make the necessary arrangements. After the Lion Heart died, Arthur was mysteriously murdered. The barons believed that John was responsible.

The new king's unpopularity increased. According to custom, he should have ruled with the co-operation of the barons. He ignored their advice, failed to give them the rewards they expected, treated them unjustly in the law courts, and generally scorned them. On trips to Ireland, he teased the noblemen about their old fashioned habits. In a more jovial mood, he used to pull their beards. John no doubt found it amusing. The Irish barons did not.

Nobody trusted John; nobody liked him. Eventually, the barons decided that he had gone too far. Either he must accept their demands for

King John hunting. The quarry was always deer; foxes were scorned by noblemen.

better treatment, or else they would rise in revolt.

On 15 June, 1215, King John and the barons met at Runnymede on the Thames near Windsor. After angry exchanges, the monarch was persuaded to put his seal on a document known as the Great Charter (or Magna Carta). All told, it contained sixty-three clauses. They affected all manner of things from standards of measurements to fish traps on the Thames. But the one that gave Magna Carta its reputation was number 39. It stated that no freeman might be imprisoned, outlawed, exiled 'or in any way destroyed . . . except by the lawful judgement of his peers or by the law of the land'.

It also insisted that nobody should be expected to pay a fine so large that it deprived him of his livelihood; that the barons had a right to be tried by their equals; and that the King himself came under the law.

But these legal safeguards did not apply only to the nobility. As the barons were quick to point out, all free men should enjoy them. They would grant them to their own men.

Reluctantly, King John agreed. Afterwards, he protested that he had done so under force. Consequently, he could not be expected to honour his pledge. It is possible to see his point of view. The barons had taken a tough line and, so far as the king was concerned, the terms were extremely harsh.

The result was civil war. John's men marched against the barons. But he did not live to see much of the fighting. In 1216, he died at Newark – probably as the result of eating too many peaches and drinking too much sweet ale.

As for the barons – they won in the end. In 1217, one year after John's death, his successor, Henry III, confirmed the terms of the Magna Carta. Justice, roughly along the lines we experience today, had at last been established in England.

Henry III no doubt knew what he was doing when he agreed to the Magna Carta. But the document must have been confusing, for he was only ten years old. His guardian and regent, William Marshall, probably explained it carefully to him – and almost certainly encouraged him. William Marshall had, as it happened, been one of the advisers to the charter's authors.

When the new king grew up, he added to the treasures of British architecture by rebuilding Westminster Abbey. Unfortunately, he did not do very much else. He certainly failed to provide the faith in royal authority that the country so badly needed. That had to wait until 1272, when Edward I came to the throne.

The Magna Carta: freedom on a piece of paper.

King John's Treasure
The barons asked the king of France for assistance – offering in return the crown to his son, Louis. French troops were landing on the Lincolnshire coast, when John was at King's Lynn. In an attempt to bring them to battle as quickly as possible, he ordered his men to take a short cut at low tide along the shore of the Wash. But there was not enough time. While the baggage train, rich with booty taken from the castles of defeated barons, was making the journey over the sands, the tide came in and swept the treasures away.

Trouble on the Frontiers

For centuries, the border between England and Scotland has run from the mouth of the Tweed to the Solway Firth. The early Scottish kings would have liked to push it southwards – to encompass Cumbria and Northumbria. The English kings insisted that the Scots should pay taxes, behave themselves, and keep their hands off northern England.

William I had conquered Scotland, but his successors were unable to keep the Scots under control. In 1174, William the Lion of Scotland marched his men across the Tweed. On a misty summer's morning, he came across a party of English knights outside Alnwick Castle. In the bad light, he mistook them for his own followers. He was captured with scarcely a struggle. Five months later, at Falaise in Normandy, he swore an oath of allegiance to Henry II. Twenty-one Scots barons were surrendered as hostages. Scotland was now firmly under the English thumb.

When Richard I came to the throne, he did not mind very much what happened, so long as he could raise money for his crusade. William paid him a substantial sum and Richard released him from his vows of obedience.

A weak king of England suited Scotland. Edward I, who came to the throne in 1272, was anything but weak. Not without reason, he became known as 'the Hammer of the Scots'. He was, however, prepared to try diplomacy. In 1286, the sovereignty of Scotland passed into the hands of the King of Norway's daughter, a little girl named Margaret. When she was older, Edward decided, she must marry his son. A ship laden with sugar loafs and gingerbread, figs and raisins, was sent to bring her from Norway to England.

Somewhere in the region of the Orkneys, a storm blew up, and poor Margaret died of seasickness. Hopes of a peaceful life between England and Scotland died with her.

There were now two contenders for the throne of Scotland: a man named John Balliol and another named Robert Bruce. Edward decided to make the choice. He picked John Balliol as most likely to fit in with his plans. As Edward had sensed, he was a weak character and he was harshly treated. But there was a limit to the amount of humiliation even he could take. In 1296, goaded by his advisers, he rebelled.

Edward promptly marched into Scotland. The revolt was crushed, and John Balliol fled to France. As a final insult, Edward took the Stone of Scone back to England with him. Seven hundred years earlier, this slab had been quarried in Ireland and brought to Scotland, where, kneeling upon it, Scottish kings had accepted their inheritance. It was, indeed, the very symbol of Scottish monarchy and independence.

The degradation was complete. But the spirit was far from crushed. Under Sir William Wallace, the Scots fought back. At Stirling in 1287 Wallace defeated an English force by springing an ambush as it was crossing a bridge.

Edward came storming northwards with his barons, his knights, and the rest of the army. Wallace was driven underground, and for the next seven years waged guerrilla warfare. In 1304, he was captured and executed.

Three years later, Robert Bruce (son of John Balliol's rival) crowned himself King of Scotland. Again Edward hurried towards the border. But now he was old and tired. Somewhere north of Carlisle, he died. Bruce could breathe more easily.

His moment of glory came in 1314. The scene, once more, was Stirling. The English forces were now under siege in the castle. Edward II attempted to relieve them. When the fighting stopped, the burn of Bannock was bridged by the corpses of dead warriors, and the English were in full flight. Scotland was free at last.

The Conquest of Wales

After the strong rule of William I, a succession of weaker Kings of England gave Wales an opportunity to fight for independence. Two men came to the fore. Both came from the country around Mount Snowdon; both were named Llywelyn.

Llywelyn the Great earned his title at a time when English affairs were badly managed, and when English kings – Richard I, John and Henry III – had other things on their minds. Llywelyn the Last had the misfortune to oppose Edward I.

The fact that Richard I spent most of his time abroad, and that John and (later) Henry III were busy with their barons, gave Llywelyn the Great freedom to unify Wales – to turn it, virtually, into a sovereign state. He married one of John's daughters, and was shrewd enough to recognize the English king as his master. At the same time, however, he ruled Wales as though it were his own. The result was that he remained in power for nearly fifty years, and died peacefully in his bed in 1240.

Llywelyn the Last was one of his illustrious namesake's three grandsons. When he came to power, Henry III was still having trouble with his

Harlech Castle, completed in 1283, was one of many garrisons established in Wales by Edward I.

barons; there seemed no reason why Wales should not continue to profit from the English monarchy's misfortunes. Llywelyn even proclaimed himself Prince of Wales, and Henry recognized him as such.

But then came Edward I. He was brilliant, brave, and determined to rule all four corners of Britain's mainland. Llywelyn must have underrated him. He refused to pay the necessary tributes; he even married the daughter of an English rebel. Llywelyn was taken to London, mocked and humiliated. When he was allowed to return, he was a very angry man.

In Wales itself, conditions were bad. The king's officials showed a marked lack of tact. New laws curbed the people's independence. By 1282, the country was in chaos. Sooner or later, there was bound to be an uprising. Llywelyn's brother, Dafydd, began it by seizing the Cheshire town of Hawarden. Llywelyn joined in. But now Edward was driving into Wales with a three pronged attack. At the same time, his fleet was cutting off the rich farmlands of Anglesey.

Llywelyn the Last died in a skirmish with a small force of knights – after he had been separated from his main force. His head was removed and displayed on a spike at Conway Castle. Dafydd was quickly captured. Edward had no mercy to offer him: he was hanged, drawn and quartered.

The uprising was over. Edward I built many castles to keep the natives in their place. The dream of independence was dead.

The Prince of Wales

Llywelyn the Last was the only Welsh Prince of Wales there has ever been. When Edward I was staying at Caernarvon in 1284, his eldest son was born. With grim humour, he told the Welsh that he would give them a new prince who 'could not speak a word of English'. Seven years later, in 1301, the future Edward II, was invested as Prince of Wales. Ever since it has been the title of the English monarch's eldest son.

Life in a Monastery

Throughout the Middle Ages, the Pope was head of the English church. The largest and most important building in any town or village was the church. Presided over by the local priest, it was more than a solemn place in which religious services were held. It was used for parish meetings – even, on certain occasions, for feasting.

As well as parish priests, there were friars and monks. The friars used to travel from place to place, preaching, comforting the sick, and hearing confessions. When the Universities at Oxford and Cambridge were founded in 1167 and 1209, they became some of the leading teachers.

The monks lived in monasteries ruled by abbots. Although their lives were dedicated to prayer and they had virtually no personal possessions, the establishments themselves became very rich. Some of them, indeed, were rather like well-run businesses. They certainly owned a great deal of land.

In the early days, the abbot used to live in the monastery – though in accommodation set apart from the monks. Later, however, the work of running the estate, giving service to the king, political concerns and so on, became too great. Many abbots withdrew from the establishments, set up their own households, and their responsibilities were taken over by priors.

A monastery and its estates were run by the monks. Some had special duties. For example, the precentor had to arrange the church services; the sacrist was in charge of the church furniture and fittings; and the cellarer looked after the supply of provisions and made sure there was always plenty to eat.

Life in a monastery was hard. The hours depended on the time of sunrise and sunset, but a fairly typical day was as follows. At 2.30 in the morning (sometimes at two o'clock) a bell roused

the monks for prayer. They remained in church, either worshipping or reading until eight o'clock – when they were allowed to go to their quarters, wash and change their shoes. Then they returned for mass.

The only substantial meal of the day was provided at 2 PM. Afterwards, they either worked or studied until 5 PM, when the bell tolled for Vespers. A hot drink followed; then another service; until, at about 7 PM, they retired to bed.

During every twenty-four hours, there were seven church services, each announced by the bell. The routine for one day was very like that of the next. It was a life that suited only a small, and very pious, proportion of the people.

At the end of the 14th century, there were about 5,000 monks in Britain. But standards were falling. Many put aside the hard religious discipline in favour of idleness. Men, who had taken vows of poverty, were now charging money for their work.

Once there was a wilderness. Then, in 1131, 12 Cistersian monks came to Rievaulx in North Yorkshire and began building an abbey. It prospered. By the middle of the century, there were 140 monks in residence assisted by 50 lay-workers. And it continued to grow; indeed, by the 15th century, it had become too large. Parts had to be pulled down. The great days of Rievaulx were coming to an end. In 1539, only 22 monks remained – the Dissolution of the Monasteries had come to North Yorkshire; the power of the abbot was spent.

Silence
The Carthusian monks lived in cells, which usually consisted of two rooms and a patch of garden. Meals from the main kitchen were brought to them, and they spent most of their time working and performing their spiritual duties on their own. The only time they went to church was for mass. But even then, no word passed between them and their fellow monks, for they had taken a vow of silence.

39

Life in a Castle

A castle was a fortified residence: the stronghold of a baron or, even, of the king. It was usually built on a mound and surrounded by a ditch or moat. The heart of the castle was the keep. This was the citadel: the focal point most strongly defended and, in a battle, the last to fall.

During a siege, and after the outer defences had fallen, the garrison fell back into the keep.

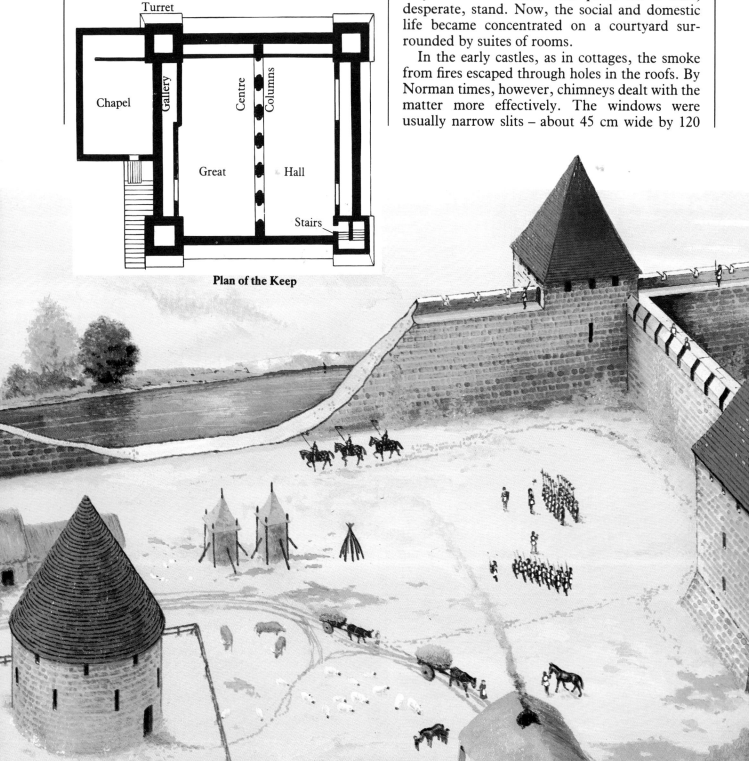

Plan of the Keep

Turret

Chapel

Gallery

Centre

Columns

Great

Hall

Stairs

Once inside, it was possible to hold out for a long time. The private apartments were situated here, offices, latrines, food stores, a well to supply water – even a chapel. There was everything necessary for a community isolated by an enemy.

But Norman keeps were gloomy places. When the likelihood of attacks by organized enemies seemed to recede – when the only dangers were peasants in revolt or outlaws from the greenwood – the lords built themselves more comfortable accommodation. The keep remained, but only as a last resort – the place for a final, desperate, stand. Now, the social and domestic life became concentrated on a courtyard surrounded by suites of rooms.

In the early castles, as in cottages, the smoke from fires escaped through holes in the roofs. By Norman times, however, chimneys dealt with the matter more effectively. The windows were usually narrow slits – about 45 cm wide by 120 cm high. Wooden shutters kept out the cold. It was not until the 14th century that glass was introduced to Britain. Even then, however, it had to be employed sparingly, for it was very expensive. The first person to enjoy its benefits was Henry III.

As well as being his stronghold in times of conflict, the castle was the key point from which a baron ruled his lands (or manors). If he controlled several manors, it might be a day's journey or more to the farthest points. Consequently, he built himself a manor house in each – so that he could spend some of his time there.

The big house was usually surrounded by farm labourers' cottages. A baron's serfs had two roles to perform. They had to cultivate their master's soil and look after his stock. In times of trouble, they had to take up arms and muster at the castle. Life for these men and their families was attended by constant hardship.

They lived in cottages built from logs or stones, with thatched roofs and floors of bare earth. Most of them were allowed to keep poultry, and had small plots of land on which they grew peas and beans. Some managed to keep a pig or a cow (about half the size of today's cattle). As for bread, it depended on the harvest.

Up at the castle, or in one of his manor houses, the lord lived well – entertained lavishly. For the peasant, who depended on his tiny patch of land for almost everything, life was much less satisfactory.

The baron dwelt in his castle: his serfs lived round about. In times of trouble, they mustered within the gates and took up arms. If things fared badly, the last place to fall was the keep (on the right of the picture).

Black Death and the Peasants' Revolt

One day in 1348, a man at Melcombe Regis (now Weymouth) in Dorset complained of a sore throat. Soon he was running a high temperature; there were swellings in his armpits and on his groin, and hard black spots appeared on his face and body. The doctor looked on helplessly, and the man died. Bubonic plague, known as the Black Death, had arrived in England.

The disease, which began in the East, was transmitted by fleas travelling on rats. It came to Europe on board an Italian merchant ship, and, by 1340, it had reached the farthermost parts of Scotland.

Once it was established, another illness, pneumonic plague, developed. This was passed on much like a present day 'flu (hence the grim nursery rhyme: 'Ring a ring of roses /A pocket full of posies/ Atish-oo, atish-oo, we all fall down'. It referred to pneumonic plague and the sneezes that were the first symptoms).

Rich people, in panic, fled from the towns – hoping for survival in the country. Some were lucky; others took the germs with them. Families, entire villages perished. And the doctors were powerless. They played with chemicals; they thought they knew much about astrology. But, for the Black Death, they had no medicine.

The epidemic lasted for two years. By the end, about one-third (it may have been half) of Britain's population had died. In Europe, 25 million perished. There were no longer enough peasants to work the land.

Until now, it had been almost impossible for a serf to move from his patch of earth; to go from a bad master to one who might be better. Now he had freedom to improve his fortunes. What was more, the promise of food and a roof were no longer enough to pay for his services. He wanted *wages*.

Many, though not all, began to receive payment for their work. Unfortunately, prices started to rise at the same time. Before long, the majority were no better off than they had been before the Black Death. Egged on by an ex-priest named John Ball, they became angry – especially when, in an attempt to stop prices rising, their wages were frozen.

The last straw was the so-called Poll Tax – levied in 1379 to pay for the 14-year old King

Richard II's useless wars with France. Every adult, no matter how much money he had, was forced to pay up. But the French continued to make a nuisance of themselves by raiding the English coast. The money, obviously, was being wasted.

In fact, there were a series of Poll Taxes. The first, in 1377, imposed a levy of 2p on everyone over the age of fifteen. Later, in 1380, it was raised to 5p a head. Commissioners travelled the country, collecting the money. In many cases, payment was long overdue. In 1381, their activities gave rise to a rumour that yet another Poll Tax was about to be levied. This was too much. The peasants rebelled. Appropriately perhaps, their first victim was one of the commissioners. The rebels were massed in two forces, one under the leadership of Jack Straw, marched on London from Brentwood in Essex. Another, under Wat Tyler, converged on the capital from Kent. On the way, Tyler's men stopped at Maidstone to liberate John Ball, who had been shut up in the local jail.

Tyler's men might have been halted at London

Right: The Black Death was the greatest killer of all. The disease arrived in England in 1348, imported by fleas that lived on rats that lived on ships. In Europe, 25 million perished; in Britain, about a third of the population died. The symptoms were fever, swellings and hard black spots.

Left: Richard II, son of the Black Prince and the Fair Maid of Kent. He died at the age of 33 – victim of the usurper Bolingbroke (later Henry IV).

Below: When the peasants marched on London, Richard took refuge in the Tower of London. But, despite the murder and mayhem, this boy king of 14 later came out to reason with the rebels.

Bridge, but rebels inside the city had lowered the drawbridge in the middle. They marched across; on the far side, they went on a rampage of murder and burning. The Archbishop of Canterbury and the Lord Treasurer had taken refuge in the Tower. The mob broke in and lynched them both. John of Gaunt's Savoy Palace was sent up in flames. Tyler did, however, manage to dissuade his men from looting.

But now the young king was riding out. In

Smithfield, he met the rebels. 'Tell me', he said, 'what you want'. Tyler began to bluster; the king remained calm. Then, suddenly, there was a scuffle. Tyler – perhaps caught up in an attack on the Lord Mayor of London – was stabbed. The mob became even angrier, but the king rode towards them. Speaking quietly, he told them to go home. He, personally, would investigate their complaints.

Impressed; perhaps feeling a little bit foolish, and robbed of their leader, the crowd dispersed. The Peasants' Revolt was over. The Poll Tax was dropped, but a promise by the king to abolish serfdom was quickly retracted. John Ball was hanged, drawn and quartered, which was certainly not part of the rebels' plans.

It is sometimes argued that the politicians had triumphed over the boy king, causing him to break his word. If this was so, it cannot have been difficult. Richard's final taunt to the peasants was, 'Villeins (another word for 'serfs' – the drudges of the soil) you are, and villeins you will remain'. It did little to suggest concern for their welfare.

The Great Cathedral

Canterbury Cathedral: it was here that the pilgrims came and prayed, and often gave princely gifts for its development.

There are many cathedrals in Britain, and it is impossible to say which is the greatest. Nor does it matter. Each is a triumph of architecture, a tribute to the survival of Christian faith.

Without a doubt, however, the best known is Canterbury. Its location marks the place where Saint Augustine brought back Christianity to England in 597 after the dark years of paganism. As a seat of learning, it produced Kings School, which is the oldest in the country. The Archbishop of Canterbury has always been the nation's senior bishop – a man who often had to combine spiritual sanctity with political cunning.

Canterbury has been a place to which pilgrims have come. The traffic was never greater than during the three centuries following the murder of Thomas Becket. Becket's death caused a sensation in Europe. People from all over the known world visited his shrine – not only commoners, but also kings and emperors. Louis VII, for example, the first French Monarch to visit Britain, made such a pilgrimage. He presented the cathedral with a gold cup and a priceless ruby from the French crown jewels.

All the pilgrims contributed something, and their gifts provided funds for rebuilding, for making the cathedral greater than ever. But perhaps the real miracle is the way in which, nowadays, it looks as if it had all been built at once. In fact, the work took place over centuries, and there were several misfortunes. The story is this . . .

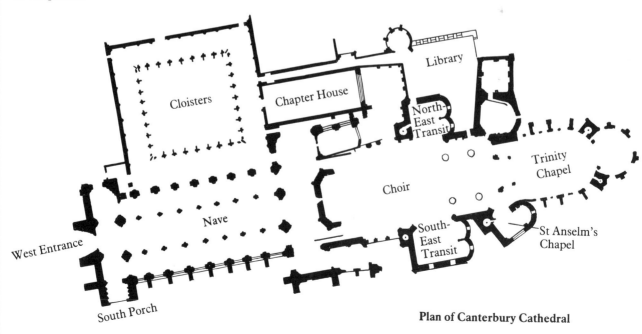

Plan of Canterbury Cathedral

The cathedral dominates Canterbury – its archbishop dominates the Church of England.

When Saint Augustine came to Canterbury in 597, the town was the capital of Ethelbert, King of Kent. With the sovereign's agreement, Augustine built a church and a Benedictine monastery.

Augustine's work survived for four centuries. But then the Danes arrived. With their harsh pagan faith, they had no time for Christian churches. They sacked most of the buildings. The few surviving parts were burned to the ground later on by a fire that broke out in 1067. Amazingly, however, the monastery survived both disasters.

William I immediately gave orders for the ruins to be rebuilt. A priest named Lanfranc took charge of the project. The new cathedral, which was double the size of the original church, was consecrated in 1130.

In 1174, four years after Thomas Becket had been killed by knights, a nearby house caught fire. Some of the sparks landed on the cathedral roof. They set it ablaze, melted the lead and destroyed the choir.

The task of repairing the damage was given to a French architect named William of Sens. He ordered stones from Caen in Normandy and they were unloaded at Fordwich – a few miles down the River Stour, which flows through Canterbury.

Alas, poor William! One day when he was up on the scaffolding, he fell off and was killed. Another architect, William the Englishman was appointed. Among other things, he was responsible for the design of the crypt (an underground vault beneath the church), which is the biggest in the world.

During the years that followed, the pilgrims came and went – each making a gift and so helping the cathedral to be made even more impressive. Among the improvements was the construction of the great tower, Bell Harry. Two hundred and thirty-five feet high, it took eight years to complete (between 1495 and 1503). It contains one bell, which is tolled only on the death of a sovereign or an archbishop.

Henry VIII completed the destruction by the Danes and that fire of 1067, when he was responsible (indirectly, at any rate) for the demolition of Saint Augustine's monastery. In its day, it had been almost as magnificent as the cathedral itself. Nowadays, only the foundations remain.

Finally, the cathedral had a narrow escape on 1 June 1942, when German aircraft bombed Canterbury. Much of the town was severely damaged, but the greatest of its buildings received only minor injuries.

45

Towns and Trade

Medieval towns were usually built at crossroads, or at points where it was possible to cross a river. They were small by today's standards – some no bigger than a large village. Their inhabitants grew crops on the town field; grazed cattle on the common pasture. In 1388, a law was passed by which journeymen and apprentices had to put down their tools at harvest time to help cut and gather in the corn.

The houses, built from wood and plaster, were crammed together. There was no sanitation, and the smell was atrocious. Not surprisingly, they were breeding grounds for the plague and other diseases.

Livestock roamed the streets (except in London, where it was forbidden. Anyone who came across a stray pig was entitled to cut its throat and take its carcass for pork.) There were no policemen and no street lighting. Anyone who went out alone after dark was asking for trouble. Admittedly, the whipping post, the stocks and the gallows stood in the square as grim reminders of punishment.

London was, and had been for some time, an important city. Ships came up the Thames; foreign merchants established themselves in big houses. Craftsmen and merchants tended to keep together, and streets were named after their trades. You can find a reminder of it today in such places as Bread Street and Leather Lane.

Merchants and craftsmen formed guilds. The guilds controlled prices (and profits); dealt with justice; looked after welfare necessities; and negotiated with the lord of the manor. They also controlled the training of apprentices and the standard of workmanship.

At first, the craftsmen's guilds were not very powerful. The workshops were small; the master, the journeyman and the apprentice all worked and ate together. Later, as industry expanded, the gap between employers and employed became larger. There were strikes for higher wages, and the guilds became the forerunners of present day trade unions.

Trade over long distances was difficult. The magnificent Roman roads had long crumbled, and the only highways were rough tracks. At sea, ships were lost in storms. Some fell victim to pirates.

But business was brisk. From East Anglia, Yorkshire and the West Country, Britain was exporting the finest wool in the world. And then there was tin from Cornwall, iron ore from the Forest of Dean, coal from Newcastle, lead from Derbyshire, and so on. The country was rich in raw materials. They paid for imported luxuries such as wine and spices, silks and satins, oranges and lemons.

A great deal of British wool used to be exported to Flanders, where it was made into cloth. But then people began to ask themselves whether this was a good idea. If the Flanders weavers could make money from British wool, why should the end product not be made in Britain? Small industries were set up. The government encouraged this enterprise by charging duty on the export of wool. It had to leave the country as bales of cloth. Inevitably, this resulted in smuggling – especially in the south-east. But the cloth trade flourished, and marked Britain's first bid to become an industrial power.

In the Middle Ages, wool meant wealth. The fortunes of Chipping Camden, Gloucestershire, were founded on this very exportable commodity. Business was transacted in the market place, shown here.

The Hundred Years War

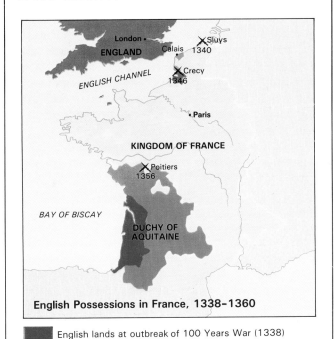

English Possessions in France, 1338–1360

■ English lands at outbreak of 100 Years War (1338)

▨ English Gains by 1360, after Treaty of Brétigny

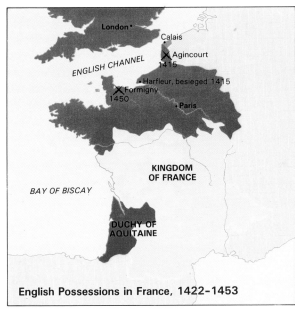

English Possessions in France, 1422–1453

▨ English Possessions at death of Henry V (1422)

▨ English Possessions at end of 100 Years War (1453)

In 1338, the English and French started a war that went on until 1453. It was called the Hundred Years War. In fact it wasn't really a hundred year war. It rumbled on spasmodically for longer than this, but the 'Hundred-and-fifteen Year War' might not sound so impressive. The original cause of it was that Edward III (1327–1377) felt that he should be King of France.

The fact that the war went on for over a century should not suggest that the fighting was continuous. It was, rather, a number of isolated campaigns; and subject to many interruptions. For example, the Black Death occurred early on, and this put a stop to operations for at least two years. Richard II took very little interest in it; and even Edward III, who started it all, had to negotiate a truce at one point – simply because he had run out of money.

Edward III's Campaigns

The first battle took place in 1340 and it was the first naval battle for a great many years. One hundred and sixty-five French ships were anchored off the Flemish harbour at Sluys. They were lashed together in four lines to prevent an attack. The English fleet of 250 vessels – led personally by Edward III – manoeuvred to windward with the sun behind them. Wooden castles had been built at the fore and after parts of each ship, and these were crowded with archers. After the first volleys had been discharged, the attack developed into a desperate hand-to-hand struggle. The French fleet was almost completely destroyed with enormous casualties. One of the rewards of victory was that, without a navy, the French were no longer able to carry out raids on the English coast.

After Sluys, Edward was in financial difficulties, and it was not until 1346 that he could afford to go campaigning once more. He landed on the French coast with a force of 10,000 English archers, 3,000 knights, 4,000 Welsh light infantry, 3,000 light cavalry, and a number of cannons. The idea was to drive inland to Paris, but he was halted on the River Somme.

On the afternoon of 26 August, 1346, his army formed up on a hillside near Crecy. It had been raining all day; but, at six o'clock, the sun came out. From his command post in a windmill, Edward waited for the French attack. He suspected that his men were outnumbered by three to one; and he must have been concerned for the 17-year-old Prince of Wales (the Black Prince), who was well to the fore. But when somebody suggested that his son should be withdrawn to safety, he shook his head. 'Let the boy win his spurs', he said. The boy won them.

The French were in too much of a hurry. Galloping uphill with the sun in their eyes, the cavalry collided with their own archers. When, at a range of 150 metres, mercenaries from Genoa let fly with their cross-bows, most of the bolts fell short. The English archers, with their six-foot longbows, bided their time. Then, when the range was right, they fired in perfect unison. Within seconds, there were fearful casualties in the French ranks.

For the English, the worst was over. Nevertheless, the French made fourteen more attempts to break through. All of them failed. Crecy cost them something like 20,000 casualties. The English losses were about 200.

From Crecy, Edward turned his attention to Calais. The town was besieged for a year. Eventually starvation caused the inhabitants to surrender. Edward insisted that the keys be brought to him by the six leading citizens – wearing nooses round their necks, ready to be hanged. But the French queen pleaded for their lives, and Edward relented.

After the Black Death, the war was resumed, with the Black Prince campaigning in France. In 1356, he fell into a trap at Poitiers; offered to surrender and was refused. It was, perhaps, as well. In the battle that followed, the French were routed, and their king taken prisoner.

Henry V's Campaigns

Two generations of sovereigns lay between Edward III and Henry V, the next English monarch to apply himself purposefully to the war. In the late summer of 1415, he captured Harfleur after a siege lasting two months. But disease and enemy action had robbed him of 3,000 men. Worried about the state of his army, he decided to make for Calais, marching at the rate of fourteen miles a day.

Outside the castle at Agincourt, he came across a French force that (as at Crecy) outnumbered the English by three to one. It had been raining. Henry's troops looked like a collection of scarecrows. They were tired, hungry, sick, clad in rags, and many of them were barefooted. But they had the courage of desperate men, especially when Henry told them the enemy had threatened to cut off two fingers from the right hand of every archer captured.

The French had to advance across a newly ploughed field, and they seemed reluctant to begin. Henry knew that his forlorn army could not exist in the field for another day without the spoils of a victory. The battle *had* to take place.

Right: Henry V – hero of Agincourt. His success was due to the skill of the English archers – and the bad luck of the French cavalry, which floundered in the mud. At one point, a false alarm caused the king to order the execution of his prisoners.

Below: Joan of Arc – a farmer's daughter who thought she heard voices from heaven. Inspired by them, she led the French troops to victory at Orleans. But, in the end, she was betrayed and burned at the stake.

Right: The scene is a French town under siege in the 100 Years War. The cannons created more fear than slaughter, but the crossbows were deadly. So, too, were the more conventional bows and arrows. The picture is taken from a manuscript prepared in about 1480.

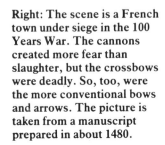

After waiting anxiously for three hours, he told his archers to move forward. When they were within 300 metres of the French troops, they let loose a volley of arrows.

Immediately, the French were stung into action. But as their knights rode towards the English, their horses were shot from under them. They fell, helplessly, into the mud. Burdened by very heavy armour, most of them were unable to get up again. The English might be less well protected, but at least they could move freely.

By midday, the French attack seemed to have spent itself. But now there were reports of trouble in the English camp at the rear. Henry ordered all the prisoners to be killed. He had, he protested, not enough men to guard them.

The king himself led the final charge of the day, which completely dispersed the French forces. When the fighting stopped, the French had lost about 10,000 dead and 30,000 wounded. The English casualties totalled no more than 300.

From Agincourt, Henry pressed on to Paris, where he married the King of France's daughter, on the understanding that he should inherit the French throne. But the French King outlived him. In 1422, Henry V died – and so did England's successes in France. The French army was given new heart by a 19-year-old girl named Joan of Arc. Bit by bit, the English were shaken loose from their conquests until only Calais remained. As for the English archers, their usefulness ended at the battle of Formigny in 1450, when the French cannon carried out dreadful punishment. Three years later, the war ended.

Shining Armour

Throughout the Middle Ages, the knight in armour was considered to be the most powerful figure on the battle field. Every ambitious lad would have liked to have been one (but, for many ambitious lads, this was impossible: to be a knight, you had to belong to the gentry). These men were heroes. Their courage and skill at fighting had to be great. They were also supposed to be good men: men who defended the weak and helpless, who looked after women and children in times of danger. The rules that governed their behaviour were known as 'chivalry'.

Edward III, especially, believed in chivalry. He founded the Order of the Garter in 1344. He created a court to make sure his knights behaved correctly, and he loved the bright colours of pageantry and tournaments.

A medieval knight and his lady.

Jousting was a sport and a preparation for war. People were apt to be badly, and sometimes mortally, wounded until rules were drawn up and blunt weapons used.

A tournament was at once a sport and a means of training knights for their role in warfare. It had been invented by the French. During the 12th century, a tournament (in this case called a *melee*) was a mock battle between two sides. Unfortunately it was more dangerous than intended. Many were killed or wounded in these events.

Later, jousting was introduced. Two knights charged each other with levelled lances. The idea was to unseat the opponent. Henry II banned jousting; Richard I allowed it – but insisted on issuing licences for tournaments; Edward III loved it. Henry II of France also enjoyed it. Perhaps he was too enthusiastic: he was killed in a bout.

Eventually, the casualty rate was reduced by the introduction of blunt weapons and a code of rules. Special arenas were built, and competitors (no one less than a knight was allowed to take part) were charged entry fees.

But there were changes afoot. While Edward III was encouraging tournaments and chivalry, he was also experimenting with the use of the cannon. Cannons needed gunpowder. The army now had gunpowder. Had the monarch thought about it, he might have realised that lances and longbows, swords and swashbuckling, were all out of date. All sorts of things, including muskets, were now possible. After the Hundred Years War, battles would never be quite the same again. But Edward III was dead long before this happened.

The Wars of the Roses

'The Wars of the Roses' is a glamorous name thought up in the 18th century for an unglamorous tale of intrigue and betrayal; of small battles fought by small forces. Indeed, the very mention of 'roses' is false. It was not until late in the wars that Yorkshire adopted the white rose as its emblem. Lancashire did not assume the red rose until some time after it was all over.

It might never have happened if, in August 1453, King Henry VI (Henry V's son and heir) had not gone mad. The mad monarch belonged to the house of Lancaster. Since Henry had no son and was obviously incapable of governing, Richard, Duke of York, the legitimate heir to the throne, proposed himself as regent.

At the last moment, and much to everyone's surprise, the Queen (Margaret of Anjou) gave birth to a son. This put an end to Richard's chances of becoming king, just as King Henry's equally unexpected return to sanity made a nonsense of his role as regent.

Reluctantly, Richard stood down. But he did not give up. Henry VI was imprisoned in the tower, but his wife raised an army. She defeated Richard of York's men at the battle of Wakefield in 1460, and had the satisfaction of seeing Richard killed. His head was chopped off, adorned with a paper crown, and put on a spike over one of the entrances to York.

The King was released from the Tower. But the supporters of York were not yet done. Their next candidate for monarch was Richard's son, Edward, Earl of March.

The two forces clashed again in a snowstorm at Towton, Yorkshire, one winter's day in 1461. The Yorkists won; Edward was acclaimed King Edward IV; Henry and his queen fled. Henry was eventually captured, but Margaret escaped to France.

In May 1471 the Yorkist and Lancastrian forces fought at Barnet, north of London. The result was an utter rout of the Lancastrians and the death of Warwick the 'King-maker'. For the next twelve years peace reigned until the death of Edward IV at the age of forty revived the struggle for power between the Houses of Lancaster and York. During the thirty years of this power squabble known as the Wars of the Roses armies were in the field for only thirteen weeks in all.

Now another figure, the Earl of Warwick (known as the 'King-maker'), came on to the scene. Suspecting Margaret of trying to get help from the French, he suggested that Edward should marry a French princess. To his surprise, Edward said that it was impossible. Secretly, he had already wedded a young lady named Elizabeth Woodville.

The 'King-maker' promptly changed sides. Margaret was now back in England, and he made a pact with her. Henry VI was released from the Tower, and Edward IV was driven out of London.

In May, 1471, everything erupted at the Battle of Barnet. Warwick was killed. Margaret was taken prisoner. Her son was put to death. Edward returned to the throne, and Henry returned to the Tower – where he was probably murdered.

As for the people of England, they calmly went about their businesses, paying as little attention as possible to the fighting. Fortunately the rival armies managed to by-pass the towns, and life was not seriously interrupted.

Richard III

When Edward IV died in 1483, he left behind him two sons, a daughter, and an ambitious widow whose maiden name had been Elizabeth Woodville. The elder boy, 13-year-old Edward, inherited the throne. His guardian was Richard, Duke of Gloucester, Edward IV's brother.

Richard had married the Earl of Warwick's daughter. It had been à wise match, for it brought him large estates in the north of England. As lieutenant-general of the North, he was the king's agent in those parts. He was honest, brave in battle, and capable of kindness. But, like most rulers, he was ruthless. Richard neither liked nor trusted his sister-in-law. Indeed, he was suspicious of the entire Woodville family. Thinking that some villainy might befall his ward, he insisted that the lad and his brother, Richard, Duke of York, should be given quarters in the Tower.

Edward V and Richard moved in – and vanished. The only evidence of their deaths is the skeletons of two boys dug up in the 17th century.

All the rest is mystery.

Since the Duke of Gloucester promptly proclaimed himself King Richard III, he was suspected of murdering the lads. He never troubled to deny the charges, but no court of justice could have convicted him. Was Richard guilty? Did he hire assassins? Or was it part of a plot to arouse popular feeling against him?

Richard III is always given the role of villain: a hunchback, who prowls wickedly through the pages of history. In fact, he was in most ways a fair ruler who did much to root out corruption, and the slight deformity which earned him the nickname 'Crouchback' was greatly exaggerated by the Tudors.

Left: Richard III with some of his advisers. Good at administration, honest and brave in battle, he was not quite the villain history has made him.

Above: Reputedly a hunchback, some say Richard's deformity was the work of artists in the pay of his enemies.

Right: The Princes in the Tower – Edward V and Richard Duke of York – are one of history's great mysteries. Were they murdered on the orders of Richard III? The only evidence is two skeletons dug up in the 17th century. Of proof, there is none.

The Clash of Arms

The quarrel between the Houses of York and Lancaster (and, therefore, the Wars of the Roses) was finally brought to an end in 1485, when Richard III was killed on the field of battle near Market Bosworth in Leicestershire. He was slain by one of the soldiers employed by Henry Tudor (soon to become Henry VII), who had recently landed at Milford Haven in Wales and had been greeted enthusiastically by many Welsh warriors.

During the fight, Richard fought well, but many of his noblemen deserted him. Afterwards, the crown of England was found lying beneath a hedge. Henry put it on. The last of the Plantagenets was dead. The Tudors had arrived.

Country Life

The intrigues and wars of the court had little effect on the average countryman's life in the Middle Ages and in Tudor times. Circumstances were much as they had always been – hard. Two bad harvests in succession added up to a famine, and peasants (or some of them) starved to death.

England's successful wool trade created prosperity for the sheep farmers. But one shepherd is enough to tend a flock, and this did nothing to help the unemployment situation. The fact was that the population had steadily increased. There were now too many people for the country's economy to support. The result was that farm labourers roamed the land, looking for work.

These men lived in cottages built of wood and mud. They owned only a few pieces of cheap furniture and some tools. Moving home was easy. The Cottage Act of 1589 insisted that, before any such building could be constructed, there had to be four acres to go with it. Before that, the law was simple. Anyone could build a cottage on common land, provided he was able to raise the roof and have a fire burning between sunset and sunrise.

A labourer and his family lived off bread and ale, peas and beans, bacon from a pig and eggs from the hens. Fresh meat was a rare luxury. The chief source was poaching. All game was protected, but many people – even clergymen – set out with dogs and nets, traps and crossbows, to hunt in the forests. With luck, a man might bring home a deer.

Since the end of serfdom, a new figure had established himself on the rural scene. This was the small farmer who owned a piece of land. By the end of the 16th century, several in south-east England were living in two-storeyed homes.

Village life was busy. In 1555, an Act was passed that made road repairs the responsibility of every parish. The outcome was that every able-bodied villager had to put in one week's work a year, unpaid, on the highways.

What with trying to earn a wage and scratching enough food for himself and his family, a farmer had little leisure. Since there were no books, and no one could read, people told stories to pass the time. Sometimes, they played dice or backgammon (the upper classes preferred chess). In the 14th century, playing cards were introduced. Out-of-doors, football – using a pig's bladder – was commonplace. There were no rules, no pitches, and no limit to the number who could

play. In the 15th century, golf became so popular in Scotland that the authorities banned it.

At certain times of year – usually on saints' days – a crowd was permitted to assemble. The result was a fair. Some of these gatherings went on for several days. The purpose was to do business. The traders brought goods: people for miles around enjoyed a shopping spree. For entertainment, there were musicians, actors, clowns and jugglers.

Many people who came to fairs would normally have been thought of as hostile. They were *outsiders*; people to be regarded with suspicion. To show that they were welcome, a large hand was often displayed on opening day. At Exeter's Lammas Fair, for example, a stuffed glove was carried on a decorated pole.

But the realities of country life could be seen in those wandering families of peasants, desperately trying to find enough food to stay alive.

A peasant woman.

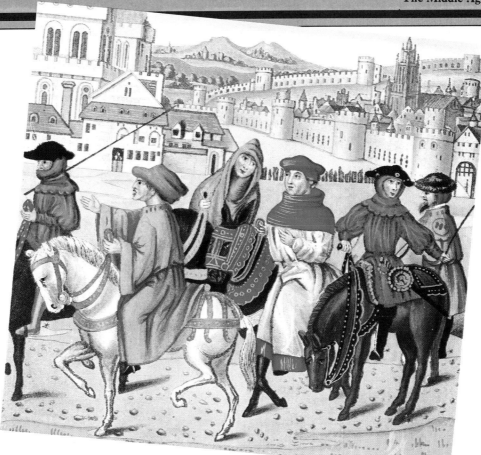

Left: In August, everyone had to turn to and gather in the harvest.

Right: The pious and not so pious pilgrims journeyed on horseback and foot to Canterbury. Chaucer told some of their stories in *The Canterbury Tales*.

Books and Education

The Christian church was the sole source of books and education. The monks used to copy out works by hand. Some – such as the gospels penned between 698 and 721 by the monks of Lindisfarne under the guidance of the bishop – were beautifully produced and illustrated. A Jarrow monk named Bede completed the *History of the English Church and People* in 731. It was the first account of the country's story since its earliest days.

So far as education was concerned, the Church was interested only in training youngsters for the priesthood. King Alfred took a more generous view. He wished that every free-born boy should be able to read. Since all the books were in Latin, he ordered them to be translated into English. He did some of the work himself – often putting in stories that were not in the originals.

As time went by, the monasteries agreed to tutor the sons of noblemen as well as future monks. Schools were built. In the 14th century, there were between three and four hundred grammar schools in Britain, and their pupils came from a much wider section of the community. Education for the mass of the population did not arrive until the 20th century. But the upper classes – and, gradually, the middle classes,

too – were learning to read.

When every book had to be copied out by hand, there were few of them and they were expensive. Most of the works were in un-rhyming verse – though Chaucer introduced rhyming couplets when he wrote the *Canterbury Tales* in 1388. This book was full of humour – a jovial, sometimes bawdy, bit of story-telling that romped along from beginning to end.

Normally stories were told in ballads, few of which were written down. People recited them – or, sometimes, chanted them. Some attempt was made to produce books by carving letters and illustrations on blocks of wood. In 1451–56, however, a citizen of Mainz in Germany named Johannes Gutenberg produced what is known as moveable type. You could assemble the letters for a book; and, when it was printed, break them up and use them again.

Gutenberg's invention came to the notice of William Caxton, an English silk merchant living in the Flanders town of Bruges. From this beginning Caxton produced the first English printing press. In 1476, he set up in business at Westminster. Between 1477 and 1491, he published nearly eighty books. Among them were romantic stories from France, translated into English.

Tudor England

When Henry VII defeated Richard III on the battlefield of Bosworth, and, according to legend, found the crown of England beneath a hedge, he started a dynasty that saw the blinkered Middle Ages transformed into an age of enlightenment. Indeed, the reign of Elizabeth I was a 'Golden Age': the age of Shakespeare, exploration and elegance.

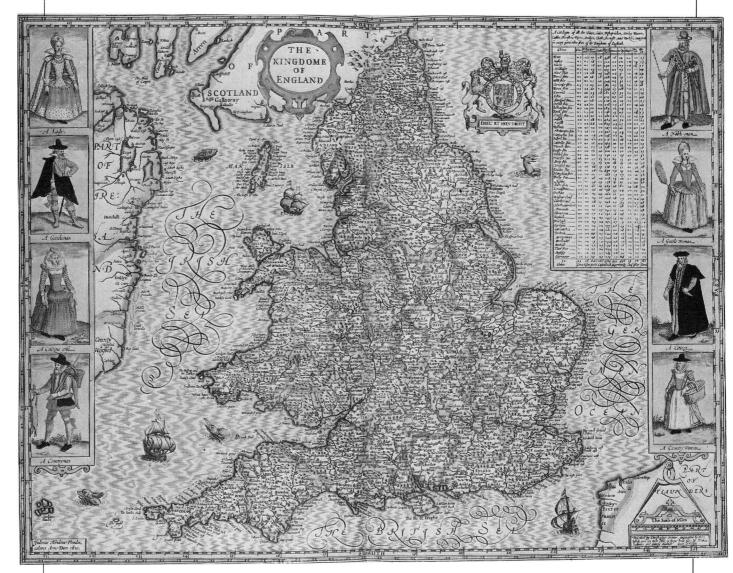

This map shows England as it was in Tudor times.

Henry VII

Henry Tudor, the first of the Tudor kings, was distantly related to the English royal family. He had been brought up in Wales by his uncle, Jasper Tudor. On the death of Henry VI, he suddenly found himself head of the House of Lancaster. But, with the Yorkist Edward IV occupying the throne, he was compelled to flee to France. It was more than his life was worth to remain in Britain.

Nevertheless, he was determined to return and to claim the crown he believed was rightfully his. When he landed at Milford Haven in 1485, he was accompanied by a small force of French soldiers. The Welsh, angry at their harsh treatment by the English, joined him – and the march to Market Bosworth began.

As a sovereign, Henry VII took life very seriously. He did not, for example, employ a court jester. On the other hand, he added to the collection of royal architecture by building a sumptuous palace for himself at Richmond.

Understandably in such treacherous times, he had a great concern for his own safety. At his coronation, he was attended by fifty archers known as the Yeomen of the Guard of our Lord the King. The Yeoman of the Guard still exist and parade on ceremonial occasions. (They should not be confused with the 'Beefeaters' at the Tower of London, who are known as 'Yeoman Warders', and who wear similar full-dress uniforms).

Henry VII was ruthless (as were all the Tudors), enjoyed the company of merchants, explorers and scholars, and was extremely shrewd. He agreed to a truce with France – in return for a substantial sum of French gold. The nobility disliked him; the middle classes loved him. But, more important than anything, he brought stability back to English government.

The Pretender
There were many intrigues during the reign of Henry VII; many claimants to the throne. The most notorious was the former page to a Yorkist lady, Perkin Warbeck. Warbeck announced that he was Richard Duke of York – that he had escaped from the Tower when his brother was killed, and that he had a right to the throne as Richard IV. The kings of France and Scotland supported him; Henry VII banished him. He landed in Cornwall in 1497 and, with a motley crowd of supporters, advanced to Exeter, where he was taken prisoner. He confessed that he was an imposter. In 1499, after an attempted escape from the Tower of London, he was hanged at Tyburn.

A King and his Wives

When 18-year-old Henry VIII succeeded his father, Henry VII, in 1509, he was hailed as Prince Charming. He was high-spirited (he had danced a jig in his underwear at his late brother's marriage to Catherine of Aragon), scholarly, had a good ear for music, and loved pageantry and feasting. After his strict father, the Court told itself, life promised to be fun.

But, as time went on, Henry developed an entirely different side to his nature. He became an irritable and ruthless tyrant. Henry badly wanted a son to succeed him. When his first wife – his brother Arthur's widow – failed to provide him with one, he demanded that his marriage should be annulled. Since he had wedded his sister-in-law, he claimed that a true marriage had never really taken place.

The Lord Chancellor and Archbishop of York, Cardinal Wolsey, was instructed to negotiate with the Pope. Wolsey failed. He was stripped of

Henry VIII came to the throne as a prince charming – handsome, athletic and musically gifted. He later grew fat, ill-tempered and embittered.

all his possessions and offices, and died soon afterwards. Perhaps he was lucky. Most of those who failed Henry ended up in the hands of the public executioner.

The plan that eventually brought about the divorce was conceived by Wolsey's secretary, a scheming, ice-cold character named Thomas Cromwell. Cromwell suggested that the Pope's consent did not matter: that Henry should break away from Rome and appoint himself head of the Church in England. Henry agreed – though he still believed in the Roman Catholic doctrine, and insisted that heretics should be burned at the stake.

The dissolution of the monasteries followed. The King's excuse was that they were badly run and that many of the abbots were conducting shady business deals. He also believed that they were siding with the Pope against him – which was not true of them all. Only two did. Another reason was, of course, that he was able to confiscate their treasures. The wealth that he acquired came in very useful. Henry, like most kings in this period of history, was nearly always hard up.

During the years that followed his parting from Catherine of Aragon, Henry married five more times. Only two of his wives brought him any happiness.

So far as foreign policy was concerned, his father had stopped warring with France. Henry, largely because he felt it might be profitable, resumed the conflict. It came to an end in 1514 when Wolsey arranged for his sister Mary to marry the ageing French king, Louis XII.

Whatever his other skills, Henry was not a good general. He had little success in his campaign against France. When, in 1513, James IV of Scotland invaded England, he was away on the Continent. It was his wife, Catherine of Aragon, who organized the campaign led by the Earl of Surrey, which defeated the Scots at Flodden Field, Northumberland.

In naval matters, the king did rather better. He founded Trinity House, extended the Royal dockyards, and encouraged the building of faster, better armed, warships. He also made Ireland into a kingdom, and did much to assist the universities.

The final verdict on Henry VIII must be that, despite the image of 'Bluff King Hal', he was an unhappy man. Most of his marriages failed. He did, admittedly, produce a son who eventually inherited the throne of England (Edward VI). But Edward was a sickly youth, he died at the age of sixteen, six years after his father's death.

The Wives

1. Catherine of Aragon: *daughter of a Spanish King, who for political reasons, married Henry's elder brother, Arthur, when the latter was fifteen years old. Arthur died in the following year. In 1509, she married Henry; later gave birth to six children. A daughter, Mary, was the only one to survive – the others were either stillborn or else died in infancy. Her inability to produce a male heir and Henry's growing infatuation for Anne Boleyn were the causes of her divorce. She died of cancer in 1536.*

2. Anne Boleyn: *had been a maid of honour to Henry's sister, Mary. Henry fell in love with her, gave her lavish presents, and asked her to become his mistress. Anne refused. After his divorce from Catherine of Aragon, he married her. She produced one daughter, Elizabeth (later Elizabeth I). Anne turned out to be a nagging wife who, he suspected, was unfaithful to him. After a quick trial for adultery, she was beheaded.*

3. Jane Seymour: *was the daughter of Sir John Seymour. She served as a lady-in-waiting to Catherine of Aragon and Anne Boleyn – was privately married to Henry on 30 May, 1536. She gave birth to the future Edward VI – a sickly boy who died at the age of sixteen. Jane died shortly after his birth – much to Henry's distress.*

4. Anne of Cleves: *was chosen by Thomas Cromwell because of her father's (John, Duke of Cleves) support of Protestantism. She was dull and ugly, and Henry detested her. He nicknamed her his 'Flanders mare'. The marriage lasted only a short time before it was annulled. Anne survived; but Thomas Cromwell was accused by the king of treason and heresy – and executed.*

5. Catherine Howard: *daughter of the Duke of Norfolk. She and Henry were secretly wedded on the day of Cromwell's execution. Soon afterwards, however, she fell in love with a courtier named Thomas Culpepper. It turned out to be one of several affairs. Culpepper was beheaded. After a confession had been forced from her, Catherine followed her lover to the block.*

6. Catherine Parr: *had already been twice widowed before she married Henry. A staunch protestant, she was good natured, capable and kind to Henry's children by his other wives. She outlived him: after his death, she married Thomas Seymour – brother of Henry's beloved Jane Seymour.*

A Royal Feast
The following is the menu from one of Henry VIII's banquets. Needless to say, not every item was eaten, but everything was available:-
First course: *Bread and soup, beef, venison, mutton, swan, capons, baked carp and fritters.*
Followed by: *jelly, spiced wine, pheasants, herons, bitterns, partridges, quails, cocks, plovers, gulls, kid, lamb, pigeons, larks, rabbits, pullets, chickens, venison paste and tarts. The drinks were beer, ale and wine.*

The New Religion

There must have been many Englishmen who, in the reign of Henry VIII, scratched their heads, and asked themselves what, exactly, *was* the country's religion. The Pope had started the trouble by refusing Henry a divorce. Thomas Cromwell had encouraged the king to decree that he, and not His Holiness in Rome, was the supreme head of the English Church.

Cromwell and the Archbishop of Canterbury, Thomas Cranmer, were the leaders of the new religion. Among other things, they introduced English Bibles into churches. It was the first opportunity that many members of the congregations had experienced of seeing – let alone reading – the holy book. Cranmer even went so far as to marry – something that Roman Catholic priests were not allowed to do. But he seems to have been uncertain of the King's attitude to this. According to one story, he kept it a secret, even to the extent of sometimes hiding his wife in a trunk. Poor Cranmer – he had cause to regret his attitude. When Mary came to the throne, he was burned at the stake as a heretic.

In various parts of the country, monasteries had been dissolved. Some said the monks deserved it. They had become rich far beyond the dreams of righteousness, slack in their duties, and ready to forgive sins in return for hard cash. But most of the monks were given pensions; some were found other employment in the

Henry VIII appointed himself head of the Church of England, defender of the faith, second only to God. At Chichester, Bishop Sherbourne begged him to confirm the charter of his cathedral (above).

Below: Cardinal Wolsey. He condoned Henry's divorce from Catherine, but the king broke him nonetheless.

church, one or two even became bishops.

Nor did it follow that the wiping out of the monasteries was carried out by Protestants. In Cornwall, for example, the men responsible were Catholics. Anyone who studied their finances could see that the monarch was not the only person to profit from the Dissolution.

Henry had certainly not abandoned the Catholic doctrine. Heretics were burned; apart from the business of the Pope, his personal beliefs were in no way altered. Nor would his people have approved of change. Had he gone too far, it might have cost him his throne.

When he died, a Council of Regency took over the care of his delicate son. Eventually, the responsibility was assumed by the Duke of Somerset, who was a staunch Protestant. The Duke introduced a new prayer book, destroyed shrines, and helped himself to the Church's wealth. He was eventually brought to ruin and execution by the Earl of Warwick, who promoted himself to Duke of Northumberland and took over the boy king's protection.

Northumberland carried Protestantism and the plundering of churches, a stage farther, and yet he was uneasy. He knew that Edward VI had not long to live; and that, most probably, he would be succeeded by Catherine of Aragon's daughter, Mary Tudor. Mary was an almost fanatical Catholic. When she came to the throne, the pomp of Rome would be restored and the flames of the heretics' fires would burn more fiercely than ever. He was right, but he miscalculated. He tried to prevent Mary coming to the throne, failed, and ended up on the scaffold.

Mary married King Philip II of Spain soon after becoming Queen, and she brought a reign of terror to England – for anyone, that is to say, who was not a Catholic. When Anne Boleyn's Protestant daughter, Elizabeth, succeeded her in 1558, the new monarch had to unravel the muddle.

In Scotland, religion had been in a similar state of confusion. French influence kept Catholicism going; but, with the accession of the Protestant Elizabeth in England, it began to wane. The process was assisted by a fiery little ex-priest named John Knox. Knox was an extremist: he disapproved of music in churches, of pictures, of all bishops, and he even abolished the Christmas festival. From the pulpit, he preached the damnation of sinners, the immorality of joy. It was a tough, humourless faith, but many Scotsmen accepted it – not least, perhaps, because Knox encouraged the downtrodden poor of Scotland to look their masters squarely in the face.

A Queen and her Enemies

When Mary died, her half-sister (Henry VIII's younger daughter) Elizabeth became Queen. She had three main problems; religion, foreign affairs and the economy. They were enough to tax the skill and patience of any sovereign. Elizabeth certainly did not solve them, she simply pushed them to one side.

Elizabeth, who had red hair, was twenty-five when she came to the throne. As she once told

Protestantism
The word 'protestant' comes from the word protest – a protest against the Roman Catholic Church. It was the idea of a German named Martin Luther. Luther, who had been a monk, found that his interpretation of the Bible was not that of the Church. Nor could he agree to the forgiveness of sins in return for money. Finally, he denied the Pope's authority completely.

A Frenchman named John Calvin who lived in Geneva was more extreme. He preached a harsh discipline, a strict way of life. The affairs of the Church, said Calvin, should not be run by bishops but by a 'presbytery', which was a committee made up of the clergy and representatives of the congregation. He inspired John Knox, and from the word 'presbyter' the Presbyterian Church was given its name.

her troops, although she had the body 'of a weak and feeble woman', she had 'the heart and stomach of a king'. As almost a Protestant (but not entirely; for example, she objected to clergymen marrying), she was, perhaps, fortunate to survive the five fearful years when her half-sister Mary ruled. But she was prudent. She devoted herself to studying, and let the world outside take care of itself.

Once the crown had been placed upon her head, she travelled about, showing herself to her people. And the people loved her. They admired her intelligence, were impressed by her personality. Most of those who had doubted were won over. Those who were not were eventually dealt with by Sir Francis Walsingham, who was, to all intents and purposes, head of her secret police.

Outside her realm, there was less enthusiasm for the new queen. The Welsh approved because she was a Tudor, and the Tudors were known to be Welsh. The Irish, still Catholics, did not. They were in the mood for rebellion. The French king would have preferred to see his daughter-in-law, Mary Stewart, on the thrones of both England and Scotland. The Spanish King Philip II, widower of half-sister Mary, was cautious. He was polite to the Queen, sometimes charming. He even considered marrying her, and converting her to the Catholic faith. Elizabeth gave him little encouragement.

The Irish were rebellious; the Spanish wary; the Scots uncertain; the French ready for intrigue. The situation was complicated still more by a young woman named Mary Stewart, daughter of Scotland's James V.

Mary had married the king of France's son and had been queen of France for less than a year. Then her husband died. She returned to Scotland; married a nobleman named Lord Darnley

and a chapter of scandals began. Mary was taking too much interest in her private secretary, a man named Rizzio. Darnley became jealous and murdered Rizzio. Some while afterwards, his house was blown up and Darnley himself was assassinated. The supposed villain was the Earl of Bothwell. Mary married Bothwell, which seemed to suggest the rumours were true.

It was at this time that John Knox was thundering on about sin from the pulpit, and he had much to say about the goings-on of Mary. She fled to England, and Elizabeth grudgingly gave her sanctuary. Elizabeth was uneasy; Walsingham even more so. Mary was Catholic. There were many who would have liked to see her on the throne.

The plots thickened. The executioners became busier than ever. A combined force of Spaniards and Italians landed in Ireland to encourage rebellion. Mary was a threat to the throne, perhaps to the very life of the queen. Elizabeth was persuaded to sign her death warrant. Mary was beheaded at Fotheringhay Castle near Peterborough in 1587.

King Philip of Spain now decided that things had gone too far. Elizabeth, it seemed, was beyond reason. He prepared to invade England. The idea (as we shall see) was a disaster. But the trouble in Ireland continued. The Earl of Essex was sent to calm things down. He failed; turned traitor; and was executed. Eventually, the Irish were subdued in 1603, when a mass migration of Protestant Scots moved into Ulster.

For the time being, the problem was over. Looking into the future, however, the cure was probably worse than the disease. For this was when the Irish troubles *really* began. Not that Queen Elizabeth had cause to worry, for she died in the same year.

Right: The murder of Mary Queen of Scots's secretary, Rizzio, by her husband Darnley set off a chain of scandal that led to her downfall and, eventually, to her execution.

Above left: Elizabeth I. She was tight-fisted, demanding, and yet she inspired a golden age in which the arts flourished and social barriers began to crumble.

Great Explorers and Seamen

Until the second half of the 16th century, the Spanish and Portuguese were the only nations that had explored the world and built empires. Britain was not considered to be a sea power at all.

But now British mariners went in search of unknown lands. In 1576, Martin Frobisher tried to find a better route to China via the northernmost parts of America. In 1582, Sir Humphrey Gilbert established an English colony in Newfoundland. Meanwhile, his half-brother, Sir Walter Raleigh, was trying to colonize Virginia (named after Queen Elizabeth I – the 'Virgin Queen') in what is now the United States. Ships from Spain and Portugal no longer had the oceans to themselves.

The Privateers

John Hawkins was a Plymouth man; a tough West Country seaman with a genius for navigation and an impudence that amounted almost to recklessness. The Spaniards and the Portuguese had, or thought they had, the monopoly of transporting African slaves to their American colonies. Hawkins saw no reason why this should continue. He fitted out a ship' and became a slaver.

If this were a crime (and Hawkins would deny that it was), it was silly not to take it a stage further. On these voyages, he began to help himself to treasure on its way to Spain in Spanish galleons. The Spanish said he was a pirate. Hawkins denied it. He was, he protested, a privateer. His vessels were private warships. Many of England's leading citizens had shares in his expeditions. In times of war, the ships made a useful addition to the fleet.

Philip II complained to Queen Elizabeth. The queen scolded, and smiled, and accepted her share of the loot. John Hawkins became a very rich man. He was eventually appointed Treasurer of the Navy.

On one of his voyages, he nearly found himself in serious trouble. His fleet of five vessels was trapped by a superior Spanish force in the Mexican port of San Juan de Ulua. Hawkins's ship, *Jesus of Lubeck*, was shot to pieces, but he made his escape in another. He managed to bring home treasure valued at £13,500, but it cost him three vessels and a good many lives.

A small ship named *Judith* also got away. She was commanded by Hawkins's cousin, a young mariner named Francis Drake.

Francis Drake (left) sailed round the world, bringing havoc to Spanish shipping on the way. At this time, people believed there was a large and rich continent at the foot of the globe (right). They called it Terra Australis Incognita – the Unknown Land of the South Wind.

Francis Drake was the son of a parson. He went to sea at the age of twelve, learning his craft from the master of an ancient vessel that traded between the Thames estuary and the Channel ports. Later, he became third officer in one of Hawkins's ships. *Judith* was his first command.

In 1577, now established as a privateer on his own account, he set off on a voyage that was to take him round the world. Officially the object was to explore the foot of the world. An Englishman named John Dee had the idea that South America was joined to a vast continent named Terra Australis Incognita (The Unknown Land of the South Wind). According to Dee's theory, it was rich in gold and silver beyond the wildest dreams. The possibility that such a trip might bring Drake into contact with treasure-laden Spanish ships (and that he would be unable to resist such temptation) cannot have been overlooked by his backers – who included the Queen herself. But, as always, they were discreet.

Drake set off from Plymouth in his flagship *Pelican* with four other vessels. On the way southwards, a gentleman member of Pelican's complement, Thomas Doughty, tried to stir up trouble. At a small port not far from the southernmost tip of South America, Doughty was tried and executed.

As Drake knew very well, this man had been employed by Sir Christopher Hatton, one of the expedition's sponsors. Sir Christopher might be angry, and he was on good terms with the queen. A word from him in the royal ear might land Drake in trouble. Prudently, he changed the name of his ship from *Pelican* to *Golden Hind*. A gold hind was the emblem of Hatton's crest.

On emerging from the Magellan Strait, the fleet ran into a storm and was scattered. *Golden Hind*, fighting for her life, came within sight of Cape Horn. The myth of the Unknown Land of the South Wind was blown away. There was nothing but gales of wind and an unfriendly black ocean.

Eventually Drake was able to resume his course; and, off the west coast of South America he and his crew seized large helpings of Spanish

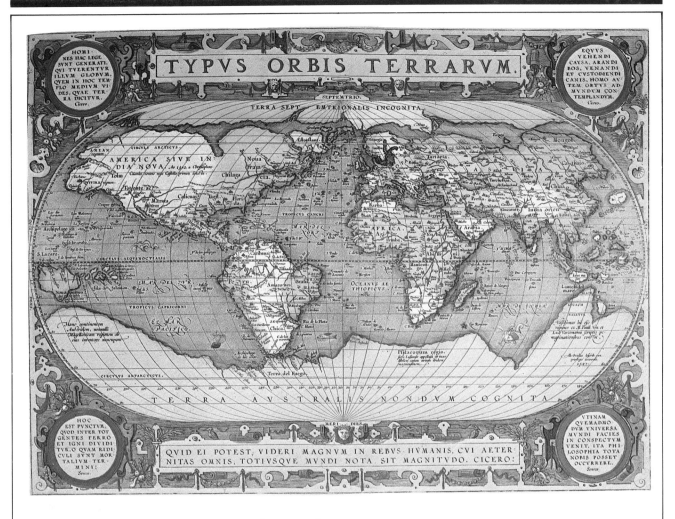

treasure. He eventually landed somewhere north of the present site of San Francisco. From there, he set course across the Pacific.

On 9 January, 1580, at eight o'clock in the evening, *Golden Hind* ran aground on a shoal near the Celebes Islands between Borneo and New Guinea. For a while it seemed as if *Golden Hind* might become a total loss. Then, almost miraculously (and just as the parson was administering the last rites to the apparently doomed crew), the wind shifted and she slid off into safety.

Golden Hind returned to Plymouth on 26 September 1580. Philip of Spain had already made vigorous complaints about Drake's action against his South American treasure ships. This time, the queen ignored them completely. Instead of rebuking Drake, she knighted him for his exploits.

It was an insult to Philip; but less so, perhaps, than Drake's action seven years later, when he sailed into Cadiz, set thirty-four Spanish ships on fire, and withdrew without any loss. He had, he proudly told his sovereign, 'singed the King of Spain's beard'.

The Spanish Armada

Philip of Spain's patience was exhausted. When the Catholic Mary Queen of Scots was beheaded, he prepared to invade England. An army under the Duke of Parma was to embark at Dunkirk and make a landing on the English coast – covered by the ships of an armada, which would sail up the Channel. The date of the operation was intended to be one day in 1587. But then a lot of things went wrong.

Drake himself was partly responsible for the postponement by his destruction of Spanish galleons in Cadiz. Then, when everything was ready in May 1588, the winds became unfavourable and many of the sailors fell sick. It was not until 15th July, that the armada's admiral, the Duke of Medina Sidonia, ordered his captains to haul up their anchors.

Off Plymouth, the armada was intercepted by the English fleet commanded by Lord Howard of Effingham and with Drake and Frobisher among its commanders. The progress up the Channel was a running fight with only small losses on either side.

But the Spaniards must have noticed that, though smaller, the English warships were much faster and more manoeuvrable than their own unwieldy galleons. What was more, their guns had a longer range. Medina Sidonia's vessels were built for combat at close quarters; for battles that belonged more properly to soldiers. Howard's on the other hand, were made for fighting sailors.

The armada reached Calais – only to find that the Duke of Parma and his army were still miles away. On 28 July, Howard sent eight blazing fire ships into their midst. The captains cut their cables in panic – and blundered into the English who were now able to fire at point blank range.

But this was not all. The wind shifted and increased to gale force. The hapless galleons (or those that had survived) were driven up the North Sea and around the north coast of Scotland. By the time the Duke of Medina Sidonia was back in Spain, he had lost 63 vessels and about 20,000 men.

Queen Elizabeth struck a special medal to commemorate the victory. It bore the Latin inscription *Deus flavit, et dissipati sunt* (God blew and they were dispersed).

The arrival of the Spanish Armada was supposed to coincide with the appearance of Spanish troops at Calais. But the army never turned up; and, in any case, the galleons had to fight their way up the Channel – beginning (above) with an engagement off Plymouth.

Below: The defeat of the Spanish Armada. The English ships were smaller but faster, and their guns had a longer range than those of the Spanish.

Life in the Elizabethan Age

Queen Elizabeth had inherited a host of economic problems. In an attempt to solve some of them, she introduced a new, re-valued, coinage. She also created a central system of wage and price control administered by Justices of the Peace. Although prices continued to rise throughout her reign, matters were kept under control until the last fifteen years, when they shot upwards. So far as her own finances were concerned, she dipped into capital and sold off parcels of land. It may have helped to settle her own difficulties; but, with less in the royal cash box, it was bound to make the lot of her successor a good deal harder.

For most people, the Elizabethan age was better than anything there had ever been before. The social classes began to mingle with each other; industry was prospering; meat found its way on to more dinner tables. Sir Walter Raleigh improved the fare in many homes when he brought back potatoes from North America. Whether his discovery of tobacco should also be applauded is, perhaps, doubtful.

On the east coast, herring fishing became an industry. Since some coastal towns in East Anglia were in decay, everything possible was done to assist it. The Queen decreed that no meat was to be eaten during Lent and on Fridays. The law, it was emphasised, was passed to benefit the fishermen and not for religious reasons. By all accounts, it was rigorously enforced. One woman, who served meat in her London tavern during Lent, was sent to the pillory. There were doubtless many other instances that have not been recorded.

German miners came to the Lake District to open up the copper mines. English iron ore was praised as the best in the world. From the Mendip Hills in Somerset came lead that was exported from Bristol. Tin was produced in innumerable small mines in Cornwall and Devon; coal, from Tyneside and Durham.

During Elizabeth's reign, the population of London increased from 100,000 to 200,000. But Britain was still mainly an agricultural community. The average town accommodated no more than about 5,000 people.

The exploits of men such as Hawkins and Drake may have suggested that Britain's role as a sea power was mainly that of robbing Spanish treasure ships. In fact, there were many harmless merchantmen going about their business, and most seamen learned their skills by serving on the

An Elizabethan lady and gentleman: elegance was everything.

A peasant and his wife: for them the dress was more modest.

colliers that brought coal from Northumberland to the Thames, or else to Holland.

But England was looking far beyond the Continent for trade. Towards the end of her reign, the ageing Elizabeth presented the Earl of Cumberland and two hundred knights with a charter of the East India Company. Intended to last for fifteen years, it exempted the company from import and export duties on its goods. It gave it concessions to export gold bullion; and it permitted six ships with a total complement of 550 men to sail to India each year.

Under this acutely intelligent sovereign, Britain discovered the world: not as an object for conquest, but as a market for exports and as a source of prosperity.

The Arts

It was as if England had suddenly woken up; as if the country had become aware of something exciting on the far side of the horizon. This did not apply only to seamen. Writers were discovering what lay in the large, unmapped land of the imagination; poets were using words as words had never been used before.

Music, too, was flourishing. The heavy hand of the Church had been lifted. The sounds, as in the singing of madrigals, had a lighter, more jaunty way with them.

This cultural re-birth (which is the meaning of Renaissance) was inspired by the monarch herself. Elizabeth wrote good Greek and Latin; spoke fluent French, Spanish and Italian; was a tolerably gifted poet and a talented musician. She enjoyed the company of men of action such as Drake, but she also liked to meet men whose traffic was in ideas.

Elizabeth loved colour. She had, it is said, 2,000 dresses. They cannot have been very comfortable to wear, but at least they were bright. Her taste became the fashion. Men dressed outrageously (or beautifully, it depends on your point of view). Short men increased their stature by wearing high heels and high hats; the fop and the dandy were not the only ones who adorned their hats with long plumes.

The world of pictorial art did not make the same progress as that of words and music. Tapestries were preferred for the decoration of walls – not least, because they helped to make a room warmer. The down-to-earth merchant had not yet developed an eye for landscape. If he bought a picture, it was usually a portrait of himself. The better works were painted by artists living on the Continent.

But everywhere there was innovation. Thomas Nashe produced the first adventure 'novel', Spenser wrote his long and complicated poem about King Arthur and *The Faerie Queen* – appropriately dedicated to Elizabeth. Indeed, it was a hint as well as a dedication: a way of suggesting that she, herself, was the 'queen' in the title.

Sir Philip Sidney, who combined the courage of a soldier with the graces of a poet, wrote his sonnets. Even Sir Walter Raleigh could turn his hand to a snatch of verse, or a history of his explorations.

But, above all things, this was the age of the theatre. There had not been a purpose-built public playhouse since the days of the Romans. Now establishments such as the Globe Theatre on the south bank of the Thames sprang up. They were tall, circular, buildings unhappily prone to catch fire. But they provided a stage for the works of such masters as Ben Jonson, Marlowe, and William Shakespeare.

Shakespeare, who owned a share in the Globe, had been born at Stratford-upon-Avon in 1564. His father traded in agricultural produce and was chamberlain of the borough. William's first job was probably as a school-master; but he soon moved on to London, where he joined the Earl of Leicester's company of players. Later, it became known as the lord chamberlain's men and (in 1603) as the king's company.

When Shakespeare joined it, the troupe was performing at the Rose Theatre. It shifted to the Curtain Theatre and, when it was opened in 1599, to the Globe. His debut as a playwright probably came about in 1592, when *Henry VI* (written in three parts) was performed. As he became more and more concerned with the writing of plays, he gave up his career as an actor – though, according to legend, he played the ghost when *Hamlet* was first performed in 1602.

Few of Shakespeare's plots were original, and yet every word he wrote seemed fresh. He had worked as an actor; he *knew* about the theatre and its audiences. He was, above all things, a great entertainer. His genius was for producing dramatic effects.

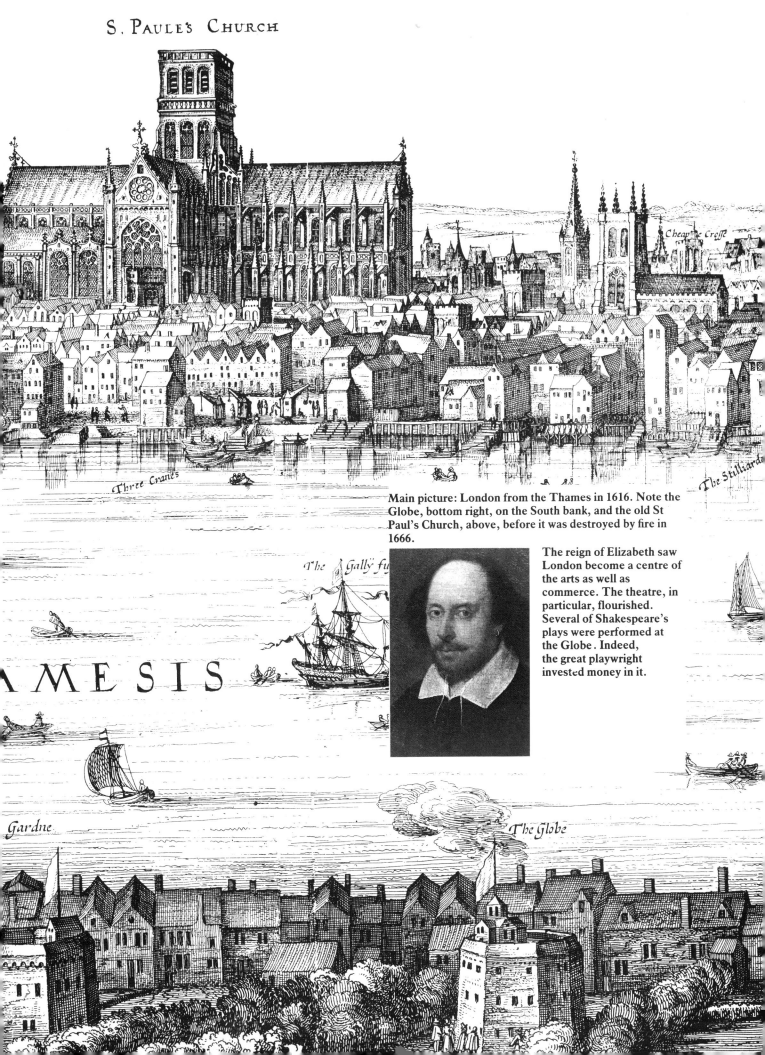

S. PAULE'S CHURCH

Three Cranes

Cheap the Cresse

The Stilliarde

The Gally fu

AMESIS

Gardne

The Globe

Main picture: London from the Thames in 1616. Note the Globe, bottom right, on the South bank, and the old St Paul's Church, above, before it was destroyed by fire in 1666.

The reign of Elizabeth saw London become a centre of the arts as well as commerce. The theatre, in particular, flourished. Several of Shakespeare's plays were performed at the Globe. Indeed, the great playwright invested money in it.

Death of a Queen

She was an aged woman, sixty-nine years old. The companions who had talked and laughed with her when she was young were all dead. Essex, who had been such a comfort in her later years, had turned against her ministers. His name was now just an addition to the long list of traitors. With sad heart, she had signed his death warrant.

She was old and she was lonely. There was no longer anyone to enjoy jokes with; to discuss a new poem or a freshly scored madrigal; no one with whom to share the gossip of the court. For some time she had been unwell. Now, on this March day in 1603, she was starting a cold. No wonder she felt miserable. Perhaps she was tired. She had served England for forty-five years. She had done all the nation could have expected of her – probably more. She had stretched herself to the limits. She may have been unpredictable; she may sometimes have shown the temper of a shrew; she was certainly ruthless when it seemed to be necessary. But she had won the love of her people; she had worked all the miracles that were necessary. She had hauled England out of a swamp of mediocrity. She had created a golden age.

The cold became worse. Soon she was very ill indeed. As she lay on her bed, she was unable to speak – unsure, perhaps, of who was with her. She had never married; she had no heir. Who, then, was to succeed her? When they asked her, she could only communicate in sign language. She seemed to be saying it should be James: James of Scotland, the only son of Mary Queen of Scots – the woman she had condemned to death. Was this an act of apology: a sign that the score was now equal and she could depart? Or was it for the very simple reason that James was a Protestant and that he really did have an hereditary claim?

Left: The wool merchants were rich and lived well. This 16th century house in Suffolk is typical of their homes.

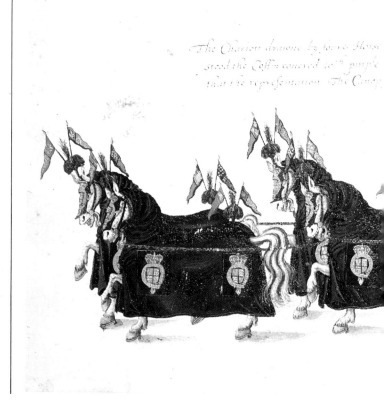

Tudor Family Tree and Stuart Succession

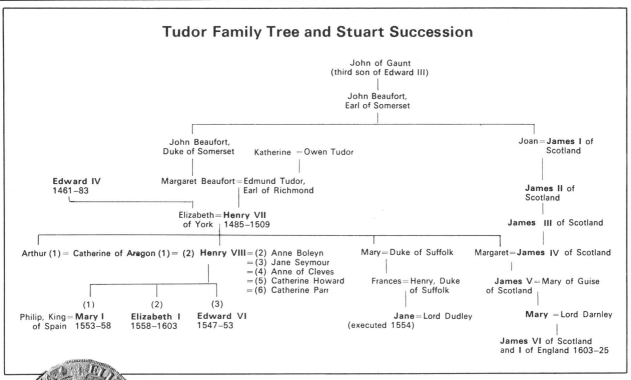

John of Gaunt
(third son of Edward III)
|
John Beaufort,
Earl of Somerset

John Beaufort, Duke of Somerset

Katherine = Owen Tudor

Joan = James I of Scotland

Edward IV 1461–83

Margaret Beaufort = Edmund Tudor, Earl of Richmond

James II of Scotland

Elizabeth of York = Henry VII 1485–1509

James III of Scotland

Arthur (1) = Catherine of Aragon (1) = (2) Henry VIII = (2) Anne Boleyn
= (3) Jane Seymour
= (4) Anne of Cleves
= (5) Catherine Howard
= (6) Catherine Parr

Mary = Duke of Suffolk

Margaret = James IV of Scotland

Frances = Henry, Duke of Suffolk

James V = Mary of Guise of Scotland

(1) Philip, King = Mary I of Spain 1553–58

(2) Elizabeth I 1558–1603

(3) Edward VI 1547–53

Jane = Lord Dudley (executed 1554)

Mary = Lord Darnley

James VI of Scotland and I of England 1603–25

Left: The gold sovereign was introduced by Henry VII. Those minted for Elizabeth I were worth 30 shillings (£1.50) each.

Below: The theatre flourished in Elizabeth's day. The Queen herself had a sense of drama. Her funeral in 1603 reflected it.

Rebellion, Restoration and Unrest

Until Charles I was executed in 1649, the king ruled by 'divine right'. But in the years of gloomy Puritan rule, Cromwell paved the way for a more democratic form of government. When Charles II regained the crown, he did so only by sanction of an elected parliament.

James I loved hunting, abhorred smoking, and handed out honours galore – in many cases undeserved. Whether Elizabeth really intended him as her successor is uncertain. Just the same, he was the first sovereign to be king of both England and Scotland.

The King from Scotland

Elizabeth I had indicated that her successor should be James VI of Scotland. No sooner was she dead, than a lady-in-waiting removed a ring from her finger. She threw it out of the bed chamber window to her husband, Sir Robert Carey, who was waiting below. Sir Robert dug his spurs into his horse and galloped off towards Edinburgh.

The ring had been a gift from James to Elizabeth. By returning it to the Scottish King, Carey hoped to convince him that the Queen was, indeed, dead – and that he was now James I of England. Using relays of horses, he made the journey in three days. James was delighted. He mistakenly believed that ruling England would be easier than governing Scotland.

On his way to London, the new King of England was accompanied by a great many hangers-on, all of whom hoped for favours from him. Few were disappointed. Elated by this happy turn of fate, James handed out knighthoods by the score. When this palled, he interrupted the journey to enjoy a morning's hunting. At last, after many more days than it had taken Sir Robert Carey to reach Edinburgh, he arrived in London.

Henry IV of France once described him as 'the wisest fool in Christendom'. The 19th century historian Macaulay was, perhaps, more accurate. Whilst agreeing that the king wrote well, he suggested that he became 'a nervous, drivelling idiot' whenever he tried to do anything.

For most of the time, he wore a dagger-proof doublet. He drank heavily, swore violently, and his personal habits were filthy. About the only vice of which he disapproved was smoking. He surrounded himself by ambitious men who had schemed and flattered their way into his favour. The more worthy men who sat in Parliament were dismissed or recalled – mostly, it seemed, according to the royal whim.

Most of the parliamentary crises had to do with money. The king, in his extravagance, needed more. Members of Parliament, in their shrewdness, refused it. Sometimes, the palaces (he had six of them) underwent economy drives, but even so royal land had to be sold. Honours no longer had to be earned; they could be bought. For payment to the king of £1,000, a man could become a baronet. When times were really hard, £10,000 could turn a commoner into an earl.

James's mother, Mary Queen of Scots, had been a Roman Catholic. She had been executed when he was twenty-one years old. His own upbringing had been as a Protestant. During his reign, Catholics, Protestants and Puritans argued endlessly about the rights of their own faiths and the wrongs of others. The burning of witches reached a record. The only way to avoid persecution was to belong to the Church of England, and to acknowledge James as second only to God.

A group of Puritans from Nottinghamshire and Lincolnshire, disgusted by the established church, decided to emigrate to America. They set off for Virginia, were driven off course and landed at Cape Cod. They named the land 'New England'; the place where they came ashore, Plymouth Rock.

North America was the goal of several adventurous spirits. Sir Walter Raleigh, the Elizabethan explorer, was accused of plotting against the king. After thirteen years in the

The Gunpowder Plot
In 1605, a group of Catholics under Robert Catesby and Thomas Percy decided to blow up the Houses of Parliament at the state opening on 5 November. The technical expert behind the plot was a man named Guido (Guy) Fawkes, who had served with the Spanish army in the Netherlands, and who understood explosives.

Barrels of gunpowder were smuggled into the cellars of the House of Lords, and Fawkes mounted guard on them. One of the conspirators, however, became worried about the safety of some Catholic friends who sat in the chamber. He wrote to one of them, warning him of the coming explosion.

His friend passed on the information; the cellars were searched – Fawkes and the gunpowder discovered. Under torture, Fawkes gave away the name of his accomplices. He and they were hanged, drawn and quartered.

Submarine
James I is said to have made a trip down the Thames from Westminster to Greenwich in a submarine. Invented by a Dutchman, the vessel certainly existed. It was powered by oars and travelled partially submerged. Reasonably fresh air was provided by two sets of bellows connected to the surface by tubes. But whether the king actually made the journey seems to be doubtful.

Tower, he was released. He had, he promised, evidence of rich gold deposits in Guiana. James agreed that he might mount an expedition, providing he gave no trouble to Spanish settlers over there. Raleigh was, perhaps, foolish. Before long, the Spanish ambassador in London was telling the king terrible tales about the brutality of him and his men. To make matters worse, they brought back no gold. On his return, Sir Walter was executed for high treason.

When James had come to the English throne in 1603, he had been full of enthusiasm. When he died in 1625, he was old, weary and disappointed. The only things for which he had shown any talent were slaughtering animals and composing attacks against tobacco smoking.

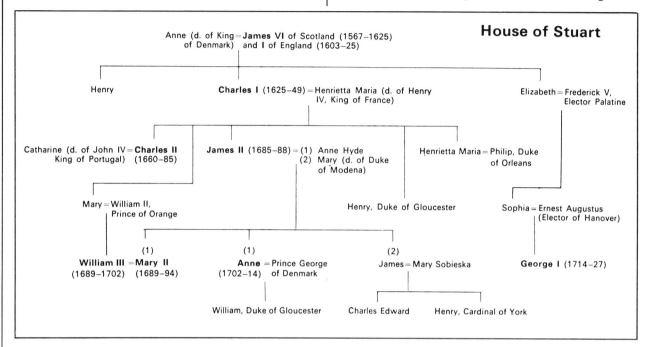

House of Stuart

Causes of Civil War

James I's eldest son, Henry, died of typhoid in 1616. Consequently the monarch was succeeded by the next-in-line, Charles. In the year of his father's death, Charles had married the King of France's daughter, Henrietta Maria. Parliament, predominantly Puritan, found little to celebrate. The new queen was a Roman Catholic; her children, she insisted, should be brought up in the Catholic faith. In fact, they were not.

The Members of Parliament, who represented the people at Westminster, regarded their new sovereign warily. Like his father, Charles soon ran into money troubles. He needed cash for his wars in Europe. When Parliament refused, it was dissolved. The king collected his own contributions. Anyone who refused to pay was either thrown into gaol, or else had his home taken over as a billet for soldiers.

Under the Duke of Buckingham's unskilled generalship, the wars achieved nothing. It came as a great relief to Parliament when, in 1628, Buckingham was murdered by a discontented naval officer named John Felton. Nevertheless, Felton was hanged.

Parliament was becoming increasingly discontented with Charles's conduct. In the same year as Buckingham's assassination, it presented the king with the so-called Petition of Right. Among the demands was that nobody should be imprisoned without cause, and that no taxes should be levied without the consent of Parliament.

Charles threw the petition out. He dissolved Parliament; and for the next eleven years ruled without its assistance. His henchmen during this period were the Archbishop of Canterbury, William Laud, and the Earl of Strafford. Laud, who was almost (but not quite) a Roman Catholic, gleefully condemned Puritans to imprisonment and mutilation. Strafford had already taken a tough line as lord deputy of Ireland. When the Scots objected to using the English prayer book in 1637 (in some cases, throwing the clergy from their pulpits) Strafford was told to deal with them. In 1639, he marched north with an ill-shod and untrained army.

Fortunately for the Scots, the troops mutinied. Parliament had to be recalled in an attempt to raise cash for a better equipped force. But the members refused to discuss the matter until their

Left: The first English
newspaper was published
in 1702. Before that,
pamphlets did the job quite
well – such as this one
illustrating the Popish Plot
of 1678. During the Civil
War pamphlets played an
important role in advancing
the Parliamentary cause.
The poet Milton was the
most famous pamphlet
writer at this time.

Below: Charles I dictates a
dispatch during the Civil
War. One of the king's
greatest weaknesses was
his indecision.

grievances were put right.

During those eleven years of personal rule, Charles had levied taxes (Ship Money) on towns and landowners to pay for his fleet. He had applied customs duties on almost all goods, and made unreasonable (often brutal) use of the Court of Star Chamber to support Archbishop Laud's rules about religion. His popularity was now at a very low ebb.

It was 1640. Parliament was recalled, dissolved, and then recalled again. After all these comings and goings, it settled down without further interruption for twenty years (which earned it the name of the Long Parliament). Perhaps the eleven-year rest had done its members good: it was certainly stronger than it had ever been.

One of its demands was that the Earl of Strafford should be executed. Charles refused. Mobs demonstrated in Whitehall; the Queen, fearful for her life, had hysterics. Charles gave in and signed the death warrant. At about the same time, Laud was thrown into prison. The angry Scots were pacified; the Irish, on the other hand, were not. They rose against the English and Scots who had exploited their lands. They killed some of their victims outright; others were stripped naked and turned out of doors to die of cold.

In London, the Long Parliament was getting some of its own way. The king was compelled to abolish the Court of Star Chamber. Even so, he refused to allow the House of Commons to approve the appointment of ministers and judges, and he turned down its demand for a share in the control of the armed forces. Funnily enough, however, he tolerated politicians meddling with the education of his own children.

The Commons were still not satisfied. In 1641, they published a document entitled the Grand Remonstrance. It contained 204 clauses. Most of them were a catalogue of royal misdeeds. They obviously hoped that Charles would get hold of a copy and read it carefully.

The King's patience was becoming exhausted. His ally, Strafford, had been beheaded. In 1645, Archbishop Laud would follow him to the executioner's block. The time had come to give the MPs a dose of their own medicine. Riding at the head of a troop of horsemen, he came to the House of Commons and demanded the arrest of five MPs and one peer. But the intended victims had been warned. As he remarked at the time, 'the birds have flown'.

Jeered by angry crowds, he withdrew. The Queen was sent off to the Continent to enlist the help of Catholic and Dutch rulers. Charles moved the rest of his family and all the court to

The queen described a Puritan politician as 'a handsome roundhead', and a new word was born. But Roundhead or Cavalier, the cartoonists could find both amusing.

York. Life in the capital had become impossible.

The situation was advancing steadily towards a state of civil war. In the summer of 1642, Charles could take no more. At the head of a conscripted army, he marched to Nottingham, where he set up the royal standard. On 23 October, near a village named Edgehill, the first battle was fought.

Roundhead versus Cavalier

During the civil war between King and Parliament, the Royalists were called Cavaliers; Parliament's troops, Roundheads. Cavalier came from the fact that their forces were renowned for their cavalry. As for Roundhead, the Queen had once met a Puritan MP with close-cut hair. She remarked that he was a 'handsome roundhead', and the name stuck.

To begin with, the average person had no very strong feelings about the rights of either side. Some of the landed gentry were apt to support Charles I; the middle classes, on the whole, backed Parliament.

Broadly speaking, the north and west of the country sided with the king. Parliament was strongest in the south and east. This meant that the Roundheads controlled London, the main ports (and, therefore, the collection of customs duties). As always, the king was hard up.

The first battle, at Edgehill, ended in a draw. It might have been a victory for Charles, if his

Naseby might have been a Royalist victory. But Prince Rupert, having defeated the Parliamentary left wing, made for the baggage camp, while Cromwell destroyed the Royalist left.

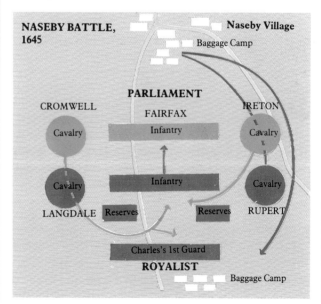

NASEBY BATTLE, 1645

Naseby Village

Baggage Camp

PARLIAMENT

CROMWELL

FAIRFAX

IRETON

Cavalry

Infantry

Cavalry

Cavalry

Infantry

Cavalry

LANGDALE

Reserves

Reserves

RUPERT

Charles's 1st Guard

ROYALIST

Baggage Camp

Oliver Cromwell: a farmer turned soldier and politician – and dictator.

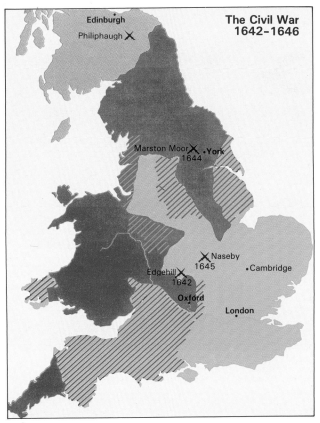

The Civil War
1642–1646

Edinburgh
Philiphaugh ✕

Marston Moor ✕ •York
1644

✕ Naseby
1645
Edgehill ✕ •Cambridge
1642
Oxford
London

☐ Areas of Parliamentary control at outbreak of war

■ Areas of Royalist control at outbreak of war

▨ Royalist gains by end of 1643 campaign

▨ Parliamentary gains by end of 1643 campaign

dashing cavalry general – Prince Rupert – had been less enthusiastic. When the Roundhead horsemen retreated, he galloped off after them. Once Rupert and his men were out of the way, Parliament's foot soldiers inflicted severe punishment on the Royalist infantry.

Afterwards, Charles should have pressed on to London. But he dithered. By the time he had made up his mind, the way was blocked. He withdrew and set up his headquarters at Oxford.

The first decisive battle was at Marston Moor in Yorkshire. It was a victory for the Roundheads, largely due to a new regiment known as Ironsides. It was a cavalry unit led by a gentleman from Huntingdon who represented Cambridge in Parliament. His name was Oliver Cromwell.

Although Marston Moor was an important success, Cromwell was not satisfied with his troops. The majority of men fighting on both sides were rogues and vagabonds. Cromwell rightly believed that professional soldiers would do better. He therefore created the New Model Army, in which the men were properly trained and equipped. Since Cromwell was a Puritan, each carried a copy of the Bible in his knapsack.

In Scotland, sympathies were divided. The Earl of Montrose supported the king; the Earl of Argyll was for Parliament. Montrose was by far

the better soldier. He routed Argyll's men at Perth and, in August 1645, occupied Glasgow.

But, two months later, Charles was in trouble. In a field near the Northamptonshire town of Naseby, his forces were smashed by Cromwell's New Model Army. Again, Prince Rupert was probably to blame. He was pursuing fleeing Roundheads, when he should have remained on the battlefield.

Afterwards, the Royalist baggage train was captured. Among the items discovered was a parcel of letters from Charles to the Queen. Most appealed for foreign support. When they were published, the effect was disastrous. Nobody much minded the King fighting Parliament. To invite the invasion of foreign troops was another matter. Sympathy for the Royalists immediately slumped.

In Scotland, at Philiphaugh (some miles south of Edinburgh), Montrose was surprised and defeated. The war was as good as over. Charles surrendered to the Scots, hoping to win them over. Instead they sold him to Parliament for £400,000.

The Commonwealth

Although the civil war was over, the problems of Cromwell and his colleagues were not. When Parliament tried to disband the army without paying its wages, the men mutinied. Cromwell stepped in. He set up an Army Council to consider reforms. Control of the armed forces was taken away from MPs.

Some members of the Long Parliament now opposed Cromwell's demands for a republic. A colonel named Thomas Pride was ordered to the House of Commons, where he threw out ninety-six members. The sixty who remained became known as the Rump Parliament.

Cromwell had once suggested that he intended to teach the King a lesson. But things had gone too far. In January, 1649, Charles I was put on trial for his life. The judges' verdict was 'Guilty'. On 30 January he was beheaded on a scaffold outside his palace in Whitehall. He conducted himself with great courage and dignity. Afterwards, on a day when snow lay thick on the ground, he was buried at Windsor. By command of the Puritans, no prayers were uttered. Shortly afterwards, the House of Lords was abolished and Britain was declared a Commonwealth.

Ever since 1641, there had been continual fighting in Ireland. Once the civil war was over, a rebellion spread across the land. Cromwell had vivid memories of the way in which Irish Catholics had butchered Protestants. He was glad of the opportunity to avenge them. Taking charge of the expedition, he left a trail of blood across the island.

In Scotland, the late king's son (the future Charles II) won support. Cromwell's general, Sir Thomas Fairfax, had been horrified by the execution of Charles I. He refused to march against the Scots, and Cromwell himself had to conduct the campaign. The prince's followers were defeated at Dunbar in 1650. Even with a price of £1,000 on his head, Charles was never given away, and eventually escaped to France.

In 1651, trying to improve the country's position as a sea power, the Rump Parliament had passed the Navigation Acts. They insisted that goods to and from British ports must be carried in British ships. This led to a war with Holland. The Dutch admiral Van Tromp lashed a broom to his flagship's mast. He would, he said, sweep the English from the seas. He failed when Admiral Blake defeated him off Portland in 1653.

In 1653, Oliver Cromwell made himself supreme ruler of Britain, calling himself 'Lord Pro-

Above: The execution of Charles I, 30 January, 1649. He was found guilty of being a 'tyrant, traitor, murderer and public enemy of the Commonwealth'. Below: Under Cromwell, all religious images which might be associated with Catholicism were destroyed.

tector', a title which he held until his death in 1658. The country, which since the execution of Charles I had been called the Commonwealth, was now known as the 'Protectorate', and a very dismal business it was. In response to Cromwell's fanatical Puritanism, theatres were closed down, dancing was forbidden, Sunday was so strictly observed that it became the gloomiest day of the week. Sometimes it seemed as if laughter itself would be outlawed. Churches were stripped of anything that, however remotely, might be associated with Catholicism. A so-called Parliamentary Visitor named William Dowsing went from place to place; smashing, burning, and generally carrying on in a manner that, at any other time, would be considered vandalism.

On Cromwell's death in 1658, his son, Richard, briefly held the title of Lord Protector. After nine months, however, the Army took over, and he went back to his life as a farmer. Parliament was expelled; courts of justice were unable to function; lawlessness and chaos were everywhere.

Fortunately, two men, General Monck and Sir Thomas Fairfax, could stand no more. The Long Parliament (or what was left of it) was recalled. In May 1660, Monck, Thomas and a committee recruited from their supporters, left for Holland. A few days later, they asked the exiled Charles II to return to Britain.

77

The Throne Restored

Charles II escaped twice from England – once via the Scilly Isles, once from a lonely creek near Brighton. When he returned from exile in 1660, good times came back too.

Charles II made his way to London in triumph. The gloom of the Protectorate was over. After more than fifteen years of Puritan rule, the country could enjoy itself once more.

The king could sometimes be deceitful, but at least he was tolerant, far more so than his members of Parliament. Twelve years after his return, he announced the Declaration of Indulgence. It was an attempt to create religious freedom. Unfortunately, in 1673, Parliament countered it by passing the Test Act, which made sure that Catholics could not hold important public positions. One result was that the king's Roman Catholic brother (who later became James II) had to resign his post of Lord High Admiral in charge of the Navy.

But the people of England had endured enough religious arguments and the suffering they so often produced. This was to be a golden age. The theatres were reopened; music was re-introduced to churches; literature flourished. Not since the days of Queen Elizabeth had there been so much to enjoy. The poet and playwright,

John Dryden, became the first Poet Laureate. Hitherto, the roles of women in plays had been performed by boys. Now actresses were employed. Even when a stubborn puritan such as John Bunyan went to prison for his beliefs, he was able to spend his time profitably. He wrote *Pilgrim's Progress*, which quickly became a best-seller.

King Charles loved richness and colour. He loved horse racing, his mistresses, extravagant meals, and watching plays. But he also encouraged the sciences. In 1662, he gave his blessing to the Royal Society for Promoting Natural Knowledge. Among its members were Isaac Newton (who worked out the law of gravity), Sir Christopher Wren (the architect), and the Rev John Flamsteed (the first Astronomer Royal).

The wars with Holland continued. The Dutch colony of New Amsterdam interrupted the line of British possessions along the eastern coast of North America. In 1664, an English force went ashore and captured the settlement. It was renamed New York.

In 1666, after a British victory off Lowestoft, the navy suffered a reverse. Samuel Pepys (better known for his diaries) was employed at the Admiralty when this happened. With the King's agreement, he produced a drastic programme of reforms. They ranged from improving the efficiency of royal dockyards to a more fair system of promotion for naval officers.

But religion, as so often, was still a source of trouble. The King professed to Church of England beliefs, though, on his death bed, he admitted that he was a Roman Catholic. His brother James openly declared himself a Catholic.

In 1678, a troublesome clergyman named Titus Oates and his scheming friend, Dr Israel Tonge, visited a London magistrate. The two men spoke of a fictitious Catholic plot to assassinate the King. His brother James was, it seemed, to be made monarch. Not long afterwards, the magistrate was found dead – murdered with his own sword. Immediately, a number of leading Catholics were executed; others were put in prison. James was compelled to flee the country. There were even attempts to involve the Queen.

One effect of this so-called Popish Plot was to strengthen the distinction between the two sides in Parliament. The King's party now became known as Tories (after a gang of Irish rogues who robbed both rich and poor), the opposition, as Whigs (after 'whiggamore' – a Scottish word for a horse-drover).

King Charles II died in 1685. His last statement was an apology for taking so long to die.

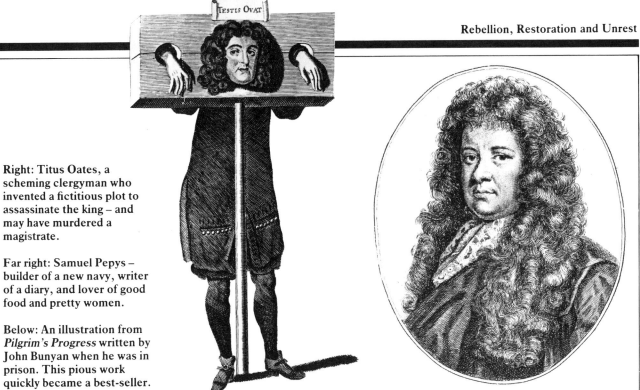

TESTIS OVAT

Right: Titus Oates, a scheming clergyman who invented a fictitious plot to assassinate the king – and may have murdered a magistrate.

Far right: Samuel Pepys – builder of a new navy, writer of a diary, and lover of good food and pretty women.

Below: An illustration from *Pilgrim's Progress* written by John Bunyan when he was in prison. This pious work quickly became a best-seller.

Plague and Fire

During the reign of Charles II, conditions in the City of London were little better than they had been in the Middle Ages. Mean and cramped houses were huddled together on either side of narrow lanes. No attempt was made to provide proper sanitation. The streets were breeding grounds for germs. In 1665, that old enemy of the British townsfolk, bubonic plague, returned again to London. It spread at such a rate that the death toll was reckoned at between three and four thousand a week.

There was no time to make coffins, nor to give the victims decent burials. Carts roamed the streets at night, their drivers calling, 'Bring out your dead'. The dead were then dumped in big burial pits on the outskirts of the city. Any house that contained a sick man or woman had to have a red cross painted on its door, and the words 'Lord have mercy upon us'.

The Lord Mayor imposed a curfew. All fit people had to be indoors by nine o'clock at night, to allow the sick to take air without passing on the infection. People took hot drinks, sniffed vinegar, burned fires, and swallowed all manner of quack remedies. But only nature could defeat the plague. It came to an end just after the New Year. The frosts, not man, killed off the germs.

The Fire of London

On 2 September, 1666, fire broke out in a baker's shop in London's Pudding Lane. Since the buildings were so close together, and a great deal of wood had been used in their construction, it spread quickly. The lanes were so narrow and twisting, that it was impossible to use proper fire-fighting equipment. In places, houses were pulled down in an attempt to create firebreaks. But for four days, the great fire blazed.

Some people stood rooted to their doorsteps in panic; others threw themselves and their possessions into the river. At last, after causing £10,730,000's worth of damage, the fire died for want of anything left to burn.

Eighty-seven churches were destroyed, 13,200 houses, all the public buildings and two prisons. Strangely enough, however, only six people died.

Afterwards, Sir Christopher Wren produced a plan for the rebuilding of London. The streets were to be wider; the buildings constructed from bricks and fitted with proper drains. Wren was allowed to build the churches he had designed, but that was all. There was not enough money to carry out his suggested improvements to the city.

In 1666, the Fire of London started in a baker's shop and spread to consume nearly all the city. More than £10 million's worth of damage was done, yet only six people were killed.

Above: James II. Left: James may have had many sins, but the greatest, in many people's view, was that of being a Catholic. During his three-year reign, Protestants lived in fear of their lives. Many were persecuted and even hanged.

Massacre

Two men tried to remove James II from the throne in 1685. Both bungled their attempts. After a voyage from Holland, the Earl of Argyll marched south from his castle at Inveraray. He reached the River Clyde, where his small army was smashed. The earl was executed.

In south-west England, Charles II's illegitimate son, the Duke of Monmouth, landed on the Dorset coast. With a rag-tag army, he was brought to battle at Sedgemoor. He and his rabble never stood a chance. The Duke was beheaded (a messy, brutal execution: the axe was blunt). His followers were rounded-up, and tried without mercy by Chief Justice Jeffreys.

Parliament was worried. Charles had at least pretended to hold Church of England views. James made no bones about the fact that he was a Roman Catholic. What was more, he insisted on a large army.

Why? He certainly didn't need it to fight that old enemy, the French. He was, as everyone knew, on excellent terms with them. Did he, then, intend to restore Roman Catholicism to Britain by force? It seemed possible.

In 1686, he won a law case that enabled him to employ Catholics in defiance of the Test Act. All was ready, it seemed, for a royal dictatorship. James's heir apparent was his daughter Mary by his first wife. Married to the Dutch Prince William of Orange, she gave Parliament no cause for

anxiety. After all, she and her husband were both Protestants. But then his second wife (a Catholic) bore him a son.

Attempts to prove that the baby was illegitimate failed. To make matters worse, James's Declarations of Indulgence in 1687 and 1688 removed the ban on Catholics holding public office. This was too much. A party of Whigs went to Holland, and invited Prince William to come to Britain. William agreed.

He landed at Torbay in Devon with a force of 14,000 men. The country welcomed him; James and his family made a hurried exit to France. This, according to Parliament, was an act of abdication. The lawful ruler was obviously William's wife, Mary. But William – a dour, ill-tempered person who suffered from asthma – was not content to remain in the background. He and Mary, he insisted, must occupy the throne as joint King and Queen. Parliament agreed.

James had not given up. With an army of seven thousand French infantrymen, he landed in Ireland. Here, surely, he would find support. But William was on the march. He defeated James on 12 July, 1690 at the River Boyne.

He and his Dutch troops were afterwards shocked at the brutality of the Irish Protestant soldiers. They massacred prisoners; even drove carriages over the wounded. It may not seem a thing to celebrate. But it is still considered a triumph by Irish Protestants – who remember it each year as Orange Day.

In Scotland, the Highlanders rebelled against

81

the new king. They even defeated his troops at the Battle of Killiecrankie. Afterwards, however, they quarrelled among themselves.

William insisted that the Highland chiefs must swear loyalty to him. Each must sign the oath by New Year's day, 1692. All but Macdonald of Glencoe obeyed. Macdonald intended to, but he was six days late. To punish the chief, a force of Campbells (Argyll's men) came to the glen. They arrived as visitors, and were treated hospitably. Two weeks later, at dead of night, they murdered thirty-six Macdonalds; burned their houses; and forced the remainder to seek sanctuary in the hills. Many died of exposure.

The Duke of Marlborough realized a soldier's two essential requirements: he needed to be well trained and adequately fed. This awareness served him well at the Battle of Blenheim in 1704, when two-thirds of the French army were wiped out.

The War of Spanish Succession

The reign of the Stuart Kings (James I, Charles I, Charles II and James II) had interrupted an English tradition – the state of being almost continually at war with France. William III, whose hatred of the French was chronic, made sure that it was revived. The opportunity occurred when the King of Spain died without an heir in 1700.

Whoever ruled Spain also governed possessions in the Low Countries, the kingdom of Naples, and the Spanish colonies in North and South America. Louis XIV proposed his grandson, Philip, as the most suitable candidate for the vacant throne. William backed the Archduke Charles of Austria.

Louis XIV struck first. He occupied territory on the Dutch frontier; banned English goods from French ports; and proclaimed James II's exiled son as James III of England.

The outcome was the War of Spanish Succession. Queen Mary II had died in 1694; her husband, William III, was killed in a riding accident in 1702. His successor and sister-in-law, Anne, was in no position to lead an army. For this, she depended on the husband of her close friend, Sarah Churchill, Duchess of Marlborough.

Marlborough was ideal for the job. Not only was he a skilled diplomat; he was also a brilliant general. Campaigning always came to a stop

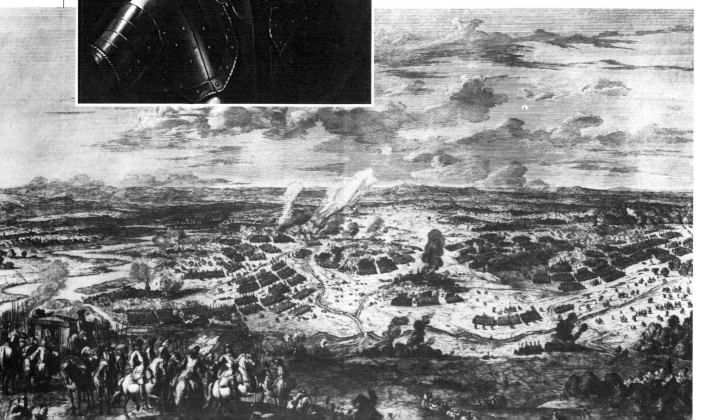

during winter months. But he used this period for training. In parties of fifty, he sent his men to the rifle ranges to practise marksmanship. They were drilled as they had never been drilled before. He drove them hard, but he also took care of their welfare. He realized that, on the march, they had to be properly fed. They should not have to worry about finding and preparing their own food. Each evening, meals were brought up in wagons, and the men could rest.

Marlborough's troops were in the Low Countries. The French had occupied Bavaria and were intending to attack Italy. Marching his men the better part of six hundred miles, the Duke won a decisive victory near the village of Blenheim in 1704.

In 1706, he was victorious again at Ramillies; in 1708 at Oudenarde; and in 1709 at Malplaquet. For the time being, France was no longer to be taken too seriously as a warlike nation.

But British businessmen, backed by the Whigs, clamoured for more war – and more battles. It was, they believed, the only way of seizing Spain's advantages in the world of trade. The Tories opposed it, and so did Jonathan Swift (author of *Gulliver's Travels*). In *The Conduct of the Allies*, Swift published a powerful attack on the hostilities.

Eventually, in 1713, peace was restored by the Treaty of Utrecht. Britain received parts of Canada, the right to hold on to Gibraltar, and the monopoly of the slave trade between Africa and South America. Marlborough was less well rewarded. Queen Anne was angry at his suggestion that he should be appointed captain-general of the Army for life. In any case the Tories had replaced his wife, Sarah, as the queen's intimate adviser by an equally formidable lady named Abigail Masham.

The Duke was dismissed from all his offices; the Treasury held up payments for the furnishing of a palace in Oxfordshire that Anne had given him after the battle of Blenheim. Perhaps they were remembering that the war in which he had fought so well cost the nation £54 million.

Act of Union

James II of England had also been James VII of Scotland. The fact that the two countries shared the same monarch may suggest that, really, they were *one* nation. But this was not so. The Scots had their own parliament, their own laws, their own religion, and their own trading problems.

The Navigation Act, for example, had been passed to protect English sea trade against the Dutch. But the same rules – that only English ships might carry goods to and from English ports – applied to the Scots. When Queen Anne came to the throne in 1702, England was prospering. Scotland was not.

In 1694, a Scotsman named William Paterson had helped to found the Bank of England. In the following year, he published details of a scheme that, he said, would rival the English East India Company. The idea was that the Scots should establish a colony on the Darien isthmus (now Panama), which joins North and South America. They would open up a trade route across the Pacific Ocean to the Far East. William III opposed the idea. Scotsmen showed their approval by investing £400,000 in the project.

It was a disaster. Two thousand colonists died either from disease, shipwreck, or by the swords of Spaniards who had settled in Darien. The investors lost all their money, which meant that thousands of Scotsmen were ruined.

How much better it might be, if England and Scotland came together completely. Queen Anne favoured the idea. After all, the Scottish parliament had every right to elect James II's son as king. English merchants were less enthusiastic. They feared the rivalry of Scottish trade. And the Scots feared the loss of their independence.

In the end, commonsense won. The Union Act passed in 1707 abolished the Scottish parliament. Instead, Scottish members were elected to the House of Commons at Westminster. On the other hand, the Act allowed the Scots to retain their own system of law, education and religion.

Newspapers

Soon after Queen Anne came to the throne, the first English newspaper was established. Known as the Daily Courant, *it marked a victory for freedom of thought. Before that, any attempts to spread the news had been heavily censored, and all printing presses had had to be registered. Two years after the* Daily Courant, *Daniel Defoe (author of* Robinson Crusoe*) founded* The Review, *a thrice weekly paper most of which he himself wrote. In 1709, Richard Steele published the first issue of* The Tatler, *which was the country's first magazine. Later, Steele joined up with Joseph Addison to publish* The Spectator – *in many ways, a forerunner of* Punch.

Queen Anne

Queen Anne was a very plump lady. During the latter part of her reign, she found it difficult to walk upstairs. To save her the trouble, a special crane was constructed. Sitting in a chair, she was hoisted to the first floor landing by means of a rope and pulley. When she died, she was buried (or so it was said) in a square coffin.

The Age of Elegance

Georgian Britain is often referred to as the 'Age of Elegance': a time of great beauty in music, fashion, architecture and art. But it was also a time of great scientific discovery and invention, which, with the coming of the Industrial Revolution, was to change the British way of life.

St Stephen's Chapel in the House of Commons in 1715 – it has changed little since then. The first man to hold the post we now call Prime Minister was a Norfolk landowner named Robert Walpole.

The First Prime Minister

Although Queen Anne became pregnant at least seventeen times, and produced six children, none of them survived childhood. When she herself died in 1714, a hush came over the court. The death of the Queen could not be announced until her successor was named. The question people asked was: who?

In fact the Elector of Hanover in Germany had been chosen back in 1701. This had been kept secret for fear the Scots might object. The new king, George I, arrived in London on a foggy day, unable to speak a word of English. Nor did he take much trouble to learn. Throughout his reign, he had difficulty in understanding his subjects. Not that it mattered much. He was more interested in the fortunes of Hanover.

The War of Spanish Succession was over; the country was deep in debt. The Tories, suspected of sympathizing with the exiled James III-that-never-was (otherwise known as the Old Pretender), soon lost power and failed to regain it. The task of getting the nation back on to its feet would have to be carried out by the Whigs. Fortunately they had just the right man to accomplish it.

In 1708, a young Norfolk landowner had joined the Whig ministry as Secretary for War. The office was, perhaps, inappropriate. Robert Walpole, for that was his name, was more interested in maintaining peace and creating plenty.

Two years later, the South Sea Company was formed. It traded in the Pacific and on the east coast of South America (dealing mostly in slaves). By 1720, it was making so much money, that its directors offered to pay off the national debt. But then something went badly wrong. The South Sea bubble (as they said) burst. The company was in ruins; and so were countless investors.

Walpole was asked to clear up the mess. He did it so well that, as First Lord of the Treasury and Chancellor of the Exchequer, he became the most powerful man in the Government. Under Walpole's guidance, the nation struggled back to prosperity. He himself made a fortune. There is no doubt that he accepted bribes, but that was not then considered wrong. It was the nature of politics in the 18th century.

Under George I and George II, not many people were able to vote at elections. Those who could seldom felt strongly about this or that party. Often they would back whichever candidate offered them the most money. Other voters

The South Sea Company collapsed after a wildly promising start. Cartoonists and ballad mongers saw the 'bursting of the bubble' as a joke. Investors who lost all their money were less amused.

were under the influence of powerful landlords. They did whatever they were told. Some wealthy and important people could control a good many seats in Parliament. When, for example, Walpole appointed the Duke of Newcastle as minister, he was also helping to assure himself a majority at the next election.

When a man was elected to Parliament, the story of bribery did not stop. If he knew the right people – offered a gift here, a favour there – his career was bound to benefit. It was an unwritten rule of politics.

King George I's stubborn refusal to learn English properly meant that he could not preside at meetings of his ministers. Since there had to be *somebody* in charge, the task fell to the most influential person present. Presently, Walpole emerged as what came to be known as 'chief minister' (later to be called Prime Minister). The system seemed to work. When George I died in 1727, the new King, George II, had a better understanding of the language. Nevertheless, Walpole continued in this role.

85

Times of War

Robert Walpole believed that trade flourished in times of peace. He was a peaceful man, a country squire who enjoyed pottering about on his Norfolk estate.

William Pitt, who was elected to Parliament in 1735, was entirely different. His grandfather had been a tough business man, who had made a fortune in the East. He shared the views of many city merchants: that prosperity came from keeping a firm hand on world trade. In nine cases out of ten, this meant war.

By 1739, Pitt's warlike speeches were beginning to overwhelm the more gentle tones of Walpole. The British Isles had been at peace for twenty-six years. Although business was booming, more and more people were clamouring for war. Their wishes were granted in 1739, when Britain threw down a challenge to Spain.

Any excuse, it seemed, would do. This was a silly one. Captain Robert Jenkins was a master mariner who carried out illegal trade with the Spanish colonies in the Caribbean. One day, his ship was stopped and searched by the crew of a Spanish coast-guard cutter. Jenkins said afterwards that one of the officers had cut off his ear. To prove it, he produced the sliced-off piece of skin in the House of Commons. The members decided that the Spanish had no right to search British ships. In 1739, Britain declared war on Spain.

It became known as the War of Jenkins Ear. Many people were delighted when it broke out. They even rang the bells of London to celebrate. But Walpole was less happy. As he listened sadly to the chimes, he said, 'They will soon wring their hands!'

But, before very long, the dispute became mixed up with another quarrel about who should occupy the throne of Austria. Most of Europe became involved. Britain and Prussia allied themselves with Austria against (as always) France. In 1743, George II commanded an army of British and Hanovarian troops in a battle at Dettingen, near Frankfurt, in Germany. It was the last time that a British king led his troops in the field.

The War of Austrian Succession at last came to an end in 1748. For the next seven years, there

Above: Clive of India – a business man and soldier who won applause for his victories and criticism for some of his deals with Indian potentates. Left: Wolfe's soldiers land at Quebec. The combined operation would have done credit to present day commandos. Right: The guard room at Calcutta – known as the 'Black Hole'. Of the 146 English prisoners, only 23 survived.

was peace. But then, in 1756, the Seven Years War broke out. It was really a struggle between Britain and France to dominate the world. Britain was allied to the Prussian monarch, Frederick the Great.

Before very long, the war had spread to India, where Britain and France were represented by the British and French East India Companies. The French supported the Indian rulers. In 1756, one of the Indian leaders confined 146 English prisoners in the military guard room at Calcutta – the 'black hole of Calcutta.' Only twenty-three escaped death from suffocation. A campaign of revenge, led by an East India Company officer named Robert Clive, came to a successful end at the Battle of Plassey in 1759.

In the Mediterranean, British troops on the island of Minorca were under siege by the French. Admiral John Byng was ordered to rescue them. But, after an indecisive fight against French warships, he withdrew to Gibraltar. Afterwards, he was court-martialled for failing to help the soldiers on Minorca. He was sentenced to death and shot on the quarter deck of HMS *Monarch*.

Britain's role in the Seven Years War was mainly as a naval power. The British fleet was stationed off the French coast – preventing enemy ships from going in or out of harbour. In 1759, an attempt by French warships to break out from Brest was defeated by Admiral Hawke at the Battle of Quiberon Bay.

The war dragged on. William Pitt, now half mad and certain he was the only person who could save Britain, became Prime Minister in 1756. One of his aims was to drive the French out of Canada and secure the fishing rights off Newfoundland. In 1759, an expedition led by General James Wolfe sailed up the St Lawrence River to Quebec. Under cover of darkness, 3,000 men were put ashore. They climbed up a steep and narrow path to the Heights of Abraham outside the city, where they defeated a much larger French force. Wolfe was killed in the fighting.

The Seven Years War ended with the Treaty of Paris in 1763. Britain received Canada and the French possessions in India; the French regained the Newfoundland fishing rights, the African trading post at Dakar and the sugar-producing islands of Guadeloupe and Martinique. Pitt, who was now out of power, was furious at the terms which, he thought, gave too much to the French.

The 'Forty-Five

Although George II probably did not know it, a young officer who was to cause him a good deal of trouble had been serving with the French forces at Dettingen. His name was Charles Edward Stuart, son of the Old Pretender and one day to be called the Young Pretender (and, also, 'Bonny Prince Charlie').

His father, James, had attempted to gain the throne of Britain in 1715, when the Earl of Mar and a number of Highland chiefs promised him support. But the whole thing fizzled out, and James returned gloomily to the Continent. In 1745, now 56 years old, he was living in Rome with his son.

Charles was dashing, handsome and brave. With the British busy fighting the War of Austrian Succession, he decided to have another try at putting his father on the throne. At first, the French promised him support. After a while, however, they seemed to lose interest.

Eventually he pawned his belongings, bought arms and presently sailed from France with two ships. The vessel carrying the weapons and ammunition was intercepted by a British warship and had to turn back. When, on 23 July, 1745, Prince Charlie landed on the Outer Hebrides, he was accompanied by only seven men – two Scots, four Irish and a solitary Englishman.

At first, nobody seemed to be enthusiastic about his plan. But Prince Charlie was very persuasive. He managed to rally the clans, won a small victory at Prestonpans and crossed the border – *en route*, he hoped, to London. He and his Highlanders reached Derby. But English troops had been withdrawn from the Continent. Three armies were now converging on his five thousand warriors. Against his own judgement, he was persuaded to retreat to Scotland.

Everything came to a tragic end on a bleak stretch of rainswept moorland named Culloden, a few miles south of Inverness. On one side were the English regiments, well-drilled and well-equipped under the generalship of George II's son – the fat and brutal Duke of Cumberland. On the other, Prince Charlie and his now very tired, hungry and ragged Highlanders were lined up. The last act of the drama occurred when, against all good sense, the Highlanders charged the English positions.

Hit by the full force of Cumberland's musket and artillery fire, few survived. The rebellion known as the 'Forty-five' was over.

With a price of £30,000 on his head, Charles Stuart escaped and was eventually taken back to France by a French frigate. The chiefs and their clansmen were less fortunate. The Duke of Cumberland lived up to his nick-name of 'the Butcher'. The wounded and prisoners were massacred. Afterwards, the homes of Highlanders were burned down, their cattle driven away, and many of their leaders executed. The wearing of tartan was banned – even the playing of bag-pipes. The system of clans was smashed and the ancient roots of Highland society were destroyed.

Above: Bonnie Prince Charlie. He was dashing, handsome, brave – but not a great general.
Left: At Culloden, the Highlanders – tired, hungry and in rags – hurled themselves to destruction when they attacked the professional English infantrymen.

Life in Georgian Britain

In the 18th century, both men and women wore wigs, those of the ladies often being very tall. Musical accomplishment was essential to any cultivated person.

For people with money, the 18th century produced many beautiful things. In the country, large houses were built in a new style of architecture, more simple than previous styles, perhaps, but certainly no less attractive. Their owners liked the surroundings to match the elegance of their homes. One man who had a great influence in this respect was Lancelot ('Capability') Brown, a landscape gardener and architect. Wealthy men employed him to work on their estates: to lay out the gardens and the parks, and generally to improve the appearances. More than 140 estates benefited from his imaginative attention.

In towns, architects such as John Nash worked their magic. London, especially, was the richer for Nash's ideas. In the early 19th century, he planned Regent Street; designed Marble Arch (it was moved from the approaches to Buckingham House – now Buckingham Palace – to its present

position in 1851) and, on George III's command, transformed Buckingham House itself into a building befitting the home of kings and queens.

Such men were artists and their work was immortal. Among those who painted pictures

A nobleman and his lady dance the minuet.

89

GLOUCESTER TERRACE.   ST. KATHERINE'S CHURCH AND HOSPITAL.

was Joshua Reynolds – who specialized in portraits. In 1768, he became the first president of the newly formed Royal Academy of Arts, housed in Burlington House, a large building in London's Piccadilly.

Not all pictures were serious, however. The cartoonists, such as James Gillray (1757–1815) had arrived. They saw the comic side of life, and delighted in making fun of important people (present day newspaper cartoonists still manage to make clowns of leading politicians and poke fun at self-important statesmen.)

But all the arts flourished during the 18th century. In the theatres, audiences applauded Sheridan's plays (*The School for Scandal*, for example) and John Gay's *The Beggar's Opera*, which caused a sensation when it was first staged.

For those who enjoyed reading, the novel became popular. You could enjoy Daniel Defoe's *Robinson Crusoe* (1719), Dean Swift's *Gulliver's Travels* (1726) and Fielding's *Tom Jones* (1749).

Up in the Lake District, William Wordsworth was busy composing his poems. In Scotland, Robert Burns (1759–1796), who began his working life as a farm labourer, eventually became a national figure. And then, at Cambridge, there was Thomas Gray, who turned down the appointment of poet laureate in 1757 – six years after he had produced *Elegy Written in a Country Churchyard*.

As for music, among the many works to be enjoyed was Handel's Messiah – which was composed in twenty-three days and first performed in Dublin in 1741. Two years later, it was produced at Covent Garden in London.

One evening during Prince Charlie's '45 Rebellion, the audience at Drury Lane – feeling, one supposes, in a patriotic mood – decided to demonstrate its loyalty to George II. Unpromp-

ted, it rose to its feet and sang a work by Thomas Arne entitled *God Save the King* (Arne also wrote *Rule Britannia!*). Thus, almost by accident, the National Anthem was established.

Some people were making war. Some were making money. Some were making a living (but only just). Some were making discoveries that, one day, would produce great inventions.

For example, a chemist in the Midlands named Joseph Priestley was conducting experiments with electricity. As a result, he found out how to isolate oxygen. A millionaire named Henry Cavendish took matters a stage further. Knowing that water was a mixture of hydrogen and oxygen, he managed to separate the hydrogen – which was used for experimental balloons.

When George III made Buckingham Palace his London home, the building was fitted with a lightning conductor. It was the invention of a scientist named Benjamin Franklin.

In 1604, the first English dictionary had been printed. When, in 1727, Nathaniel Bailey published another edition of his *Complete English Dictionary*, it was the first book of its kind to contain pictures. Dr Samuel Johnson – writer, poet and wit – published *A Dictionary of the English Language* in 1755. The doctor illustrated the use of words by quotations; but – more important – he helped to standardize spelling.

Town and Country

The 18th century was, indeed, full of new ideas. But, walking through parts of London (which now had a population of one million), it would have been hard to believe it. Sir Christopher Wren's plans for re-building the city had come to nothing. The streets were still mean and narrow. There were no drains, no lamps, and no police-

CUMBERLAND TERRACE.

men. Crime and violence abounded. Many of the villains escaped. For those who were caught, the penalties were harsh. Life in the prisons was appalling; many crimes carried the death penalty; flogging and branding were commonplace; and some villains were transported to America.

A favourite outing for many families was to Tyburn (now Marble Arch) where public hangings could be seen. Or, to make a change, it was possible to watch the flogging of soldiers in St James's Park.

Tempers sometimes erupted. In 1715, the Riot Act had been passed. If more than twelve people remained together for one hour after being ordered by a magistrate to disperse, they were guilty of a crime. But this did not put a stop to such things. In 1736, a mob turned out in Edinburgh to demonstrate at the execution of a smuggler. A captain of the guard named Robert Porteous opened fire and caused casualties. Porteous was condemned for murder; but, later, he was reprieved. Some of his fellow prisoners disagreed with the new verdict. They dragged Porteous from his cell and lynched him.

In the country, gangs of smugglers controlled large areas near the coast. But, for ordinary country people, life was much as it had been for many, many years. At certain times of year, a man worked in the fields from dawn until dusk. Nevertheless, he found time to manufacture his own tools and (if he had a small piece of land of his own) build fences. His wife made the family's clothes; brewed beer and baked bread. Even the children were given jobs, such as scaring away birds and combing wool.

For most people, it would be a long time before the new ideas of the scientists and philosophers had any effect on the standard of everyday life.

Cumberland Terrace, part of architect John Nash's bold design for Regent's Park and Regent Street.

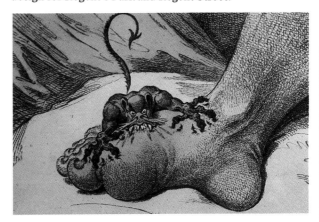

Above: Gout was the curse of the wealthy classes. Cartoonist Gillray found it a laughing matter. Its victims did not.
Below: Watching a public execution was among the popular pastimes of the day. So many crimes were punished by death, that the gallows were apt to be crowded.

The Industrial Revolution

Coalbrookdale, Shropshire, in 1777. Here, the first iron steam engine cylinder was cast; the first iron railway laid.

The 18th century saw the beginning of a complete change in the British way of life. The inventions of engineers such as Watt and Boulton were eventually to transform Britain from an agricultural community into the world's leading industrial power.

At the beginning of the 18th century, coal had been produced from surface seams. As these ran out, it became necessary to dig mines. The trouble was that they were liable to flooding. There had to be pumps to keep the water out.

In 1698, Thomas Savery (known as 'the Miners' Friend') patented the first steam engine for industrial purposes. It was not very efficient, but it served to drive the vital pumps. Three years later, an engineer named Thomas Newcomen produced a better version. But there was still plenty of room for improvement.

The man who achieved it was an instrument maker at Glasgow University named James Watt. One day in 1765, Watt was studying a model of Newcomen's engine, when he suddenly realized what was wrong with it. He went to work on the design; and, ten years later, he went into partnership with a Birmingham hardware merchant named Matthew Boulton. They built a factory and in 1775 sold their first steam engine to Whitbread's brewery in London. It cost £100, and replaced twenty-four horses that worked, six

at a time, on a treadmill. Since it cost £40 per horse per year to stable and feed the animals, the new invention obviously improved the profits.

For many years, the spinning of cotton had been carried out in cottages. It provided farm workers' wives with much needed extra income.

In the middle of the century, a Preston barber named Richard Arkwright had an idea for a better spinning machine. He became so absorbed by it, that he began to neglect his other work. His wife disapproved. Afraid of the poverty she felt must come, she smashed all his models. This was too much. Arkwright was a patient man, but now he left his wife, gave up cutting hair, and moved to Nottingham. Before long, he had built a machine that would spin a stronger thread than had ever been produced before.

But Arkwright's spinning machine was too heavy to be operated by hand. At first he employed horses to drive it; later, he used a water wheel. It needed a factory – not a cottage.

One day Arkwright was visited by a clergyman named James Hargreaves. He, too, was interested in weaving. In a way, he acted as a link between Arkwright and James Watt, for the machine he produced was powered by a steam engine.

Communications

The roads seemed to have been neglected ever since the Romans departed. It took seven days to travel from London to Edinburgh by stage coach, and the journey was far from comfortable.

But – for goods, at any rate – an alternative method became available: canals. Britain's first long distance canal was a length of 18½ miles in Northern Ireland. It took thirteen years to build, and was opened in 1742.

In 1759, the third Duke of Bridgewater was having problems transporting to Manchester the coal mined on his estate – a distance of seven miles. The answer, he decided, was to build a canal. He entrusted the design of it to James Brindley.

Since water cannot be made to travel uphill, locks (rather like lifts) had been introduced to take the boats from one level to another. But Brindley had a more daring idea. He drove the canal to its destination in a straight line without any locks at all. Using teams of mostly Irish labourers (they called them 'navigators', hence the word 'navvy') he raised it up on embankments, built tunnels to carry it through hills; and even produced an aqueduct to enable it to cross the River Irwell.

By the end of the century, Britain's canal

system was growing rapidly. One industrialist who invested in it was the pottery manufacturer, Josiah Wedgewood. A journey by inland water way was quicker than by road; the cost was less and the smooth progress over water did not damage the goods. Wedgewood had seen too many of his wares smashed to bits by waggons jolting along rutted roads.

Right: James Watt improved the design of steam engines and invented a means by which they could turn wheels.

Below: Samuel Crompton's spinning frame (or 'mule') increased the output of the cotton mills. But the workers feared redundancy. For the distribution of industry's goods, a great canal network spread across Britain (bottom). Locks enabled barges to cope with gradients. Tunnels took them through hills.

The Battle of Princeton in 1777 centred on the university's buildings. The main hall changed hands three times – and it was here the fight ended with a defeat for the British.

Rebellion in America

By the middle of the 18th century, the population of Britain was about seven million. Over on the eastern seaboard of America, there were two million settlers. A lot had happened since the day in 1620 when the Pilgrim Fathers stepped ashore at Plymouth Rock. New York, Boston and Philadelphia had been built. They were now fine cities, comparable to any place in Britain.

Although London was three thousand miles away across the Atlantic, the American colonists had to pay taxes to the government. Goods to and from the colonies had to be carried in British ships, and all American exports – no matter where they might be going – had to pass through England.

Not surprisingly, the settlers objected to this. Why, they asked, should they pay taxes when they were not represented in Parliament? In 1770, there were riots in Boston. Worried about the possibility of a full scale rebellion, the British government cancelled all taxes *except the duty on tea.*

It was not enough. On 16 December, 1773, an East India Company ship docked at Boston with a consignment of tea. Suddenly, a party of settlers – disguised as Red Indians – swarmed aboard the vessel and threw the cargo into the harbour. The British government immediately demanded that the Company must receive £15,000 as compensation. Otherwise, the port would be closed for shipping.

By the following year, the colonists were practising drill and hiding supplies of arms. When a British force marched out of Boston to destroy a secret arsenal in the village of Concord, it was ambushed at Lexington on the way back. The first shots had been fired in the American War of Independence.

At first, the rebels were an unruly mob distinguished only by good marksmanship. Many of them deserted at harvest time and went home to work on their farms. But, under the leadership of George Washington, they were gradually transformed into an efficient army. The turning point came in 1777, when a British force, marching south from Canada under General Burgoyne, was cut off at Saratoga and wiped out. Next year, France came into the war on the side of the Americans.

By 1781, part of the British forces under General Henry Clinton was bottled up in New York – confronted by a Franco-American army commanded by Washington. Many miles to the south, another British formation led by Lord Cornwallis was marching through North Carolina on its way to Washington's home state, Virginia. The two were out of touch: Clinton was far from sure what, exactly, Cornwallis was doing.

At last a message got through. Cornwallis was instructed to halt his advance and take up a defensive position. He chose the port of Yorktown, largely because he expected that supplies could easily reach him.

Everything now depended on the fleet. Unfortunately, the admiral in command of it blundered. He was outmanoeuvred by a formation of French warships led by Admiral de Grasse. Smashed by shells, their crews suffering serious casualties; the British ships had to limp back to New York to refit.

Cornwallis and his men were now completely cut off. When they tried to escape, they failed. They were suffering from illness, starvation and lack of ammunition. On 17 October, 1781, Cornwallis surrendered. British control of North America was over. The United States was a land of its own.

The State of the Empire

When, at the end of the 18th century, King George III looked at a map of the world, he must have been happy. It was covered with splashes of colour denoting his overseas possessions. Admittedly the defeat of his army in North America had cost him those colonies. But, before the settlers began their fight for independence, an Admiralty surveyor named James Cook had already (and unknowingly) done something to repair the damage to come.

Cook had. charted the St Lawrence river in Canada, making it possible for General Wolfe to reach Quebec. In 1768, the Royal Society asked him to carry out work in the South Seas. In his ship *Endeavour*, he discovered the position of New Zealand and then went on to explore the east coast of Australia. In 1770, he named it New South Wales, and claimed it for Britain. When he returned home, he wrote a report – suggesting that it might be colonized.

The American colonies had long been a dumping ground for British criminals. When they achieved independence, this became impossible. Where, then, could they be sent? Somebody in Westminster remembered New South Wales. In 1788, the first shipload of convicts was disembarked at Botany Bay, and a penal settlement was established.

The purpose of an empire was not, however, to reduce the population of British gaols. Just as wars were fought to make money, so were these scattered possessions intended to produce

George III was frequently ridiculed. This caricature was entitled 'Temperance'. In fact, the king's tastes really were moderate by the standards of the day.

wealth. In matters of law and order, the colonists were allowed to run things their own way. The East India Company, for example, ruled its territories with its own officials – and even had its own army and navy. But so far as trade was concerned, everything belonged to Britain.

No matter whether the colonists were buying, selling or shipping, the British Government (and British businessmen) profited. As a source of cheap raw materials, these overseas possessions were invaluable. As a market for the products of the growing factories in Great Britain, they were no less important.

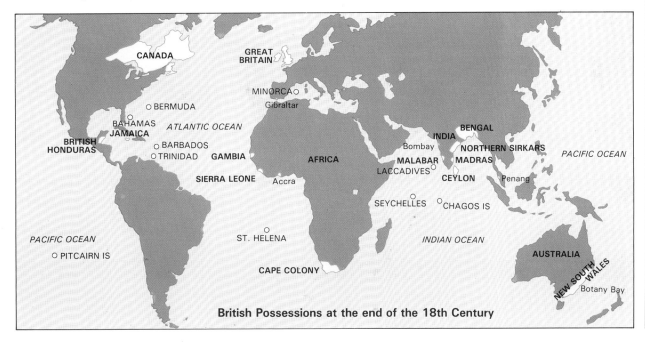

British Possessions at the end of the 18th Century

Bloodshed in Europe

People seemed to be waking up; scratching their heads thoughtfully, and asking questions. Things had been done in this or that way for a great many years. But was it the *right* way?

An economist named Adam Smith argued that all customs duties should be abolished, and that nations should trade freely with one another. In religion, a preacher named John Wesley questioned the Church of England's teaching. Ministers banned him from their pulpits. During the next fifty years, Wesley travelled a quarter of a million miles, delivered 40,000 sermons and built 350 Methodist chapels. Among the things people liked about his services were the hymns his brother Charles composed.

In 1784, the son of William Pitt (now Earl of Chatham) became Prime Minister at the age of twenty-four. Apart from a short period between 1801 and 1804, he remained in office until his death in 1806. The younger Pitt was strong, wise, and ready to accept new ideas. It was just as well, for the reigning sovereign, King George III, was going mad. In 1787, he mistook an oak tree in Windsor Park for the King of Prussia.

On the other side of the English Channel, the King of France, Louis XVI, was an absolute monarch – a ruler much as Charles I had tried to be – and who, like Charles, was usually in a chaotic state financially. But the French had watched the rebellion of the British colonists in America. Encouraged by its success, they decided to have one of their own.

On 14 July, 1789, mobs broke into the Bastille prison in Paris; released the inmates and helped themselves to the supply of arms. Led by fanatics, the new regime declared the country a republic and condemned anyone who opposed it (which meant nearly all the aristocracy) to die on the guillotine. In 1793, the king and his wife, Marie Antoinette, were both beheaded.

One might have imagined that the French had seen enough bloodshed. But, in that same year, the new government declared war on England. British troops were defeated in Holland; a force that attacked French possessions in the West Indies was driven off.

But worse was to come. In 1796, a former corporal in the French army named Napoleon Bonaparte took charge. By allying himself with Spain and occupying Italy, he forced the British out of the Mediterranean.

In Britain things were bad. There were mutinies in the Navy. A poor harvest had created great hardship. Even attempts to make peace with France were turned down. But then the tide of misfortune suddenly turned.

Below: Nelson first distinguished himself at the Battle of Cape St Vincent in 1797. Breaking many rules, he cut the Spanish fleet in half, making a British victory certain.

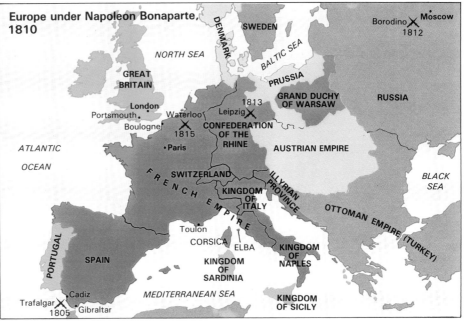

Europe under Napoleon Bonaparte, 1810

Britain and Dependent States

Napoleon's Empire

Napoleon's Allies

SWEDEN

DENMARK

BALTIC SEA

NORTH SEA

GREAT BRITAIN

PRUSSIA

Borodino × Moscow 1812

London

Portsmouth

Boulogne

Waterloo ×
1815

Leipzig × 1813

GRAND DUCHY OF WARSAW

RUSSIA

ATLANTIC OCEAN

Paris

CONFEDERATION OF THE RHINE

AUSTRIAN EMPIRE

SWITZERLAND

ILLYRIAN PROVINCE

BLACK SEA

FRENCH EMPIRE

KINGDOM OF ITALY

OTTOMAN EMPIRE (TURKEY)

Toulon

CORSICA

ELBA

PORTUGAL

SPAIN

KINGDOM OF SARDINIA

KINGDOM OF NAPLES

Cadiz

Trafalgar ×
1805

Gibraltar

MEDITERRANEAN SEA

KINGDOM OF SICILY

On 14 February, 1797, a force of British ships led by Admiral John Jervis smashed the Spanish fleet off Cape St Vincent. The hero of the action was a young captain named Horatio Nelson. Nelson's conduct had been so impressive, that he was given charge of an attempt to break back into the Mediterranean. In 1798, he came across the French ships that had carried Napoleon's troops into Egypt. His guns opened fire: the French were utterly defeated in an action that became known as the Battle of the Nile.

In 1810, Napoleon's domination of Europe was at its height. He had occupied country after country, and, in many cases, left his relatives in charge. But in 1812 he made a fatal mistake. His armies marched on Moscow.

The Napoleonic Wars

Napoleon Bonaparte – supreme general and ruler of France – was determined to invade England. He massed a large army at Boulogne and assembled a collection of boats and rafts. But, before he could attack, he *had* to have control of the Channel. This meant defeating the Royal Navy.

His nearest force of warships was at Brest, but it was unable to leave port. Just beyond the horizon, a British fleet under the command of Admiral Cornwallis was waiting. If the French ships put to sea, they would sail into almost certain destruction. Somehow, the squadron at Brest had to be helped. The man to do it was Admiral Pierre Villeneuve, who was at Toulon.

Villeneuve and his ships slipped out of port when the British Mediterranean fleet (under Lord Nelson) was replenishing its supplies of water. At the approaches to the Channel, however, the way was blocked by Cornwallis. Villeneuve turned about and put in at Cadiz, where he joined forces with the Spanish navy.

Eventually, goaded by Napoleon, he put to sea once more. At the Battle of Trafalgar on 21 October, 1805, he met up with Nelson's fleet. During the battle, Nelson was killed. Villeneuve was taken prisoner. The French force was smashed, and Napoleon's chances of invading

England gone for ever.

But, in Europe, Napoleon was conquering one country after another. In 1808, he proclaimed his brother, Joseph, as King of Spain. The Spanish rebelled, and asked Britain for help. A force commanded by Sir Arthur Wellesley (later Duke of Wellington) arrived from Portsmouth and the Peninsular War began.

Napoleon himself was too busy elsewhere to lead the French troops in Spain. Although his forces outnumbered the British, they never managed to overwhelm them. For five years, Wellesley pinned down French units Napoleon badly needed elsewhere.

The conquest of Europe by France had been a serious blow to British trade. The only market left for British goods was Russia. This, Napoleon decided, would have to be stopped. In 1812, he led his Grand Army eastwards.

The campaign was a disaster. After a victory at Borodino, Napoleon reached Moscow. But, shortly after his men entered the city, a fire broke out and three-quarters of the buildings were destroyed. At almost the same time, guerrilla forces began to harass his lines of communication. The Russian army was still intact, and the Tsar showed no sign of asking for peace.

To hold on was impossible. With the first snowflakes of winter falling, Napoleon began to retreat. During this awful journey, when intense cold and shortage of supplies added to the other perils, five-sixths of the Grand Army perished. The final blow came at the Battle of Leipzig in 1813, when it was defeated by a combined force of Austrians, Prussians and Russians.

Meanwhile, things were going badly in Spain. Wellesley's troops inflicted two crushing defeats on Napoleon's brother Joseph; by 1814, the British were pouring into France.

The war was over, Napoleon abdicated and went into exile on the Mediterranean island of Elba. He remained there for one hundred days. Then he escaped; returned to Paris in triumph and assembled another army.

On 18 June, 1815, it clashed with an army led by the Duke of Wellington, which had taken up a position outside the village of Waterloo in Belgium. It was, as the Duke of Wellington afterwards admitted, a 'near run thing'. But Wellington's infantry repulsed the French cavalry; and, at just the right moment, Prussian forces commanded by Marshal Blucher came to the Duke's assistance.

This time there could be no coming back for Napoleon. He was exiled to St Helena in the South Atlantic, where he died six years later.

Above: Napoleon – the former French corporal who set Europe ablaze.

Right: The Duke of Wellington admitted that Waterloo was a 'near run thing'. But the British infantry stood firm. The French cavalry was beaten back – and the Prussians arrived in time to save the day. After his defeat, Napoleon was transported aboard HMS *Bellerophon* to exile on St Helena. He died six years later.

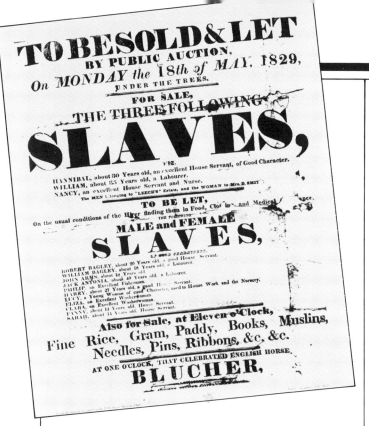

TO BE SOLD & LET
BY PUBLIC AUCTION,
On MONDAY the 18th of MAY, 1829,
UNDER THE TREES.
FOR SALE,
THE THREE FOLLOWING
SLAVES,
VIZ.
HANNIBAL, about 30 Years old, an excellent House Servant, of Good Character.
WILLIAM, about 35 Years old, a Labourer.
NANCY, an excellent House Servant and Nurse.
The MEN belonging to "LEECH'S" Estate, and the WOMAN to Mrs. D. SMIT

TO BE LET,
On the usual conditions of the Hirer finding them in Food, Clothing and Medical ...
THE FOLLOWING
MALE and FEMALE
SLAVES,

ROBERT BAGLEY, about 20 Years old, a good House Servant.
WILLIAM BAGLEY, about 18 Years old.
JOHN ARMS, about 18 Years old, a Labourer.
JACK ANTONIA, about 40 Years old, a Labourer.
PHILIP, an Excellent Fisherman.
HARRY, about 27 Years old, a good House Servant, used to House Work and the Nursery.
LUCY, a Young Woman of good Character, used to House Work and the Nursery.
ELIZA, an Excellent Washerwoman.
CLARA, an Excellent Washerwoman.
FANNY, about 14 Years old, House Servant.
SARAH, about 14 Years old, House Servant.

Also for Sale, at Eleven o'Clock,
Fine Rice, Gram, Paddy, Books, Muslins,
Needles, Pins, Ribbons, &c. &c.
AT ONE O'CLOCK, THAT CELEBRATED ENGLISH HORSE,
BLUCHER,

Fear of Poverty

At the beginning of the 19th century, a group of reformers, led by an MP from Hull named William Wilberforce, was busy persuading the rulers of Britain to abolish slavery. In 1807, Parliament passed an act suppressing the trade. It was a beginning. But, in Britain itself, a new dark age had descended on working people in the north and midlands. It was not far removed from the very slavery that Wilberforce was fighting.

The events of the French Revolution had created fear in Britain. If any such thing occurred here, the upper and middle classes believed, it was bound to succeed. After all, there were still no policemen to maintain law and order.

Consequently, the coming together of workmen – whether for political or economic reasons – was forbidden. Trade unions were banned; there was (or seemed to be) no way in which the people could protest.

And they had much to protest about. The steam engines of Boulton and Watt and the new textile machinery were doing the work of hundreds of employees. In Yorkshire, Lancashire and Nottinghamshire, there was high unemployment – and, in some cases, starvation. Those who remained in jobs were paid miserable wages and made to work unreasonably long hours.

But people did protest. According to legend (there was probably nothing in it), a Leicestershire lad named Ned Lud had flown into a rage one day. He smashed a machine that manufactured stockings. Afterwards, when anyone broke a piece of machinery, people used to say, 'Ned Lud did it'. This gave the name to a movement known as the Luddites. Its members rebelled, often violently, against the coming of factories – and the new inventions that were putting people out of work.

The Luddites were particularly active in 1816. That year, too, there were riots in Spa Fields, London. In 1817, workers from Manchester factories marched towards London. They were clad in blankets – hence their name, 'Blanketeers.' They were stopped on the way and turned back.

But the most tragic event took place in 1819, when Manchester factory workers gathered in St Peter's Field to hear an orator named Henry Hunt. The local magistrates became alarmed. Troopers of the Manchester and Cheshire Yeomanry (spare time horse soldiers) were

ordered to arrest Hunt. But the Yeomanry was unable to handle the situation and regular soldiers were sent in to protect them. In the confusion, eleven people were killed and hundreds injured.

Afterwards, the so-called Six Acts were passed by Parliament. Seditious meetings were to be dispersed; any publication that could be used for propaganda against the government was taxed (newspapers already carried stamp duty); justice had to be administered promptly; civilians were not allowed to be trained in the use of arms; and Justices of the Peace were authorized to seize arms in counties where disturbances were likely to take place.

Factory Walls

The walls of the dark factories were closing in on the poor. The machines turned; the smoke poured from chimneys; the business men prospered; and people suffered.

The building of machinery created a need for more iron. Iron ore and coal could often be found in the same area. In the Midlands, acre upon acre of green fields were transformed into the 'Black Country'. But it was really no blacker than similar districts in Yorkshire, Lancashire and South Wales.

In the rural areas, new agricultural methods had carved the countryside up into a neat pattern of rectangular fields, each surrounded by a hedge. It improved food production, but there was little place in this scheme for the peasant and his small holding. To add to the problem the population of the countryside was increasing by leaps and bounds. There was just not enough work. Farm labourers and their families set off for the growing industrial towns in search of employment. The end of the wars against Napoleon meant that a large army was no longer necessary. Half-a-million soldiers were disbanded. They, too, made for the cities looking for jobs.

In cotton mills, women and children provided the cheapest labour. In a stuffy, overcrowded, atmosphere they toiled away for twelve hours a day. Nothing, it seemed, was beyond the conscience of the new employers, drunk with sudden wealth and greedy for more. In coal mines, women and children (some aged five) could be seen dragging trucks. In the potteries, young boys laboured for fifteen hours a day. As for the men; thousands were unemployed. With women and children to be hired for a few pence a week, nobody seemed to want them.

There were, of course, exceptions. A Welshman named Robert Owen rose to become manager of some cotton mills. He refused to employ youngsters under the age of ten, and he forbade his factory foremen to beat the workers with leather straps. He shortened working hours: even established schools for little children.

In 1802, Robert Peel the elder (father of the statesman who founded Britain's police force) succeeded in passing the first Factory Act. Among the items in it was one stating that apprentices were not to work more than a twelve-hour day. In 1824, the Act banning trade unions was scrapped. Nine years later, another Factory Act appointed inspectors to oversee improvements in working conditions. At last there was a gleam of hope. But a very long time was to pass before conditions became really tolerable.

Top left: Slaves were human merchandise – to be sold to the highest bidder.

Right: Children were regarded as cheap labour. Few employers had any scruples about them. The hours were long and the work exhausting.

Left: The Peterloo Massacre in Manchester. Lives were lost and hundreds injured when the Yeomanry blundered and the regulars over-reacted.

Above: Completed in 1830, the Liverpool-Manchester Railway marked the start of a new age of travel. The conditions were informal.

Below: I. K. Brunel – the great engineer who built the Great Western line, and then steamships to cross the Atlantic.

Right: One of Brunel's greatest creations was the steamship *Great Britain*. It has now been restored and can be seen at Bristol.

The Railways Arrive

When the 18th century melted into the 19th, steam engines were already being used in several factories. They had not, however, been employed in transport. The first sign that they might have a wider application appeared on the River Clyde one day in 1802. In the face of a strong wind, a small steamboat named *Charlotte Dundas* successfully towed a couple of barges.

In the following year, Londoners caught their first glimpse of a steam locomotive, when an engine built by a Cornish mining engineer named Robert Trevithick chuffed along the road between Holborn and Paddington. In 1808, Trevithick brought the railway age a degree closer by building a circular track on the site of what is now Euston Station. The public was offered rides at 2½p a head.

There was nothing new about the idea of railways. Trucks, running along wooden rails and towed by horses, had been used in at least one coal mine during the days of Queen Elizabeth I. Indeed, the early steam locomotives were built to haul coal from the pits. The idea that they

might be used to transport passengers came later.

By 1814, William Hedley's famous *Puffing Billy* was living up to its name at a colliery in Northumberland. In 1825, the first public railway was opened between Stockton and Darlington. It inspired the formation of the first railway company (the Liverpool and Manchester) in 1830. Unfortunately the Liverpool and Manchester's opening day ceremonies were spoilt when a retired cabinet minister, William Huskisson (he had been President of the Board of Trade), was run over and killed.

To make sure of having the best possible locomotive, the company held a competition. Four engines took part – only one of them (George Stephenson's Rocket) completed the tests without breaking down. What was more, *Rocket* was able to travel at the fantastic speed of 30 miles an hour. Nothing like it had ever been seen before.

Roads, canals, all the existing means of transport, suddenly became out of date. Railway fever began to grip the land. Armies of Irish navvies advanced across the country, building cuttings, tunnels and embankments, and laying down mile upon mile of track. By 1843, there were 2,000 miles of permanent way in use; thirty years later, the figure was 14,000 miles.

At sea, the early promise shown by *Charlotte Dundas* had been developed. By 1838, there were two steamships on the North Atlantic service – a vessel named *Sirius* and the better-known *Great Western*, designed by Isambard Kingdom Brunel. Having built the Great Western Railway to Bristol, Brunel had decided there was no reason why the route should not be extended by ship to New York.

The early trains were unreliable. Locomotives broke down, and the rails were subject to faults. Passengers were divided into first, second and third classes. Those who bought third class tickets travelled in open trucks. The journey was horribly uncomfortable, especially when going through the dark, smoke-filled tunnels.

Nevertheless, it was an enormous step forward. Only comparatively rich people had been able to travel by stage coaches. Now, with carriages and trucks trailing behind them, steam locomotives offered a means of making long trips that even the poor could use. They were no longer confined to their villages and towns. They could go to wherever they could afford.

103

The Victorian Era

*The long reign of Queen Victoria saw
the rise of Britain to the zenith of its power
as the 'workshop of the world', undisputed ruler of
the seas, and proud possessor of an empire
embracing one quarter of the world,
with roots in every continent.*

Queen Victoria's coronation marked the beginning of an era of prosperity and power.

Queen Victoria Comes to the Throne

On a spring day in 1819, a coach could be seen rattling on its way from the German town of Amorsbach to England. The driver was the Duke of Kent. His wife, crammed into the back with an assortment of pets and luggage, was pregnant. Although the couple's home was at Amorsbach, the Duke was determined that the baby should be born in London.

Although the Duke of Kent was only fourth in line to the throne, he had high hopes for his child's future. A very superstitious man, he remembered the words of a gipsy fortune teller he had once consulted while on military service in Gilbraltar. She had told him that he would become the father of a great queen. He believed her. It was only right, he decided, that a future sovereign should be born in the capital. Eventually, after a hard journey, the Duke and Duchess arrived at Kensington Palace. Four weeks later, the Duchess gave birth to a baby daughter. She was named Victoria.

George III was still on the throne – though now completely insane. Consequently, the monarchy was in the hands of his eldest son, George (later George IV) – who had been proclaimed Prince Regent. He would eventually inherit the crown. On his death, it would either pass to his daughter, Princess Charlotte – or else to his brother, William. There was nothing to suggest that the gipsy's prophesy might come true. But Charlotte died in childbirth, and her baby was still-born. William did become King (as William IV), but he did not produce an heir. The gipsy had been right – though the Duke of Kent, who died of a chill in 1820, was never to know.

William IV died at Windsor early in the morning of 19 June, 1837. Immediately afterwards, the Archbishop of Canterbury, the Lord Chancellor, and the royal physician hurried from the King's deathbed to Kensington Palace. Victoria must be told at once that she was now Queen of England.

They arrived at 5 AM. Strangely, for men on such an important mission, it was some time before they could rouse a servant. Eventually, they were shown inside. The Duchess of Kent came downstairs. Victoria, she said, was still asleep. Perhaps she could be wakened up? The Duchess agreed. One hour later, the young Queen – with a dressing gown draped over her nightdress – made her entrance.

George IV had been Prince Regent from 1812 till 1820. As king, he reigned for 10 years. He had once been handsome and charming. By the time he was 30, he had gone to seed.

Until now, Victoria had always slept in her mother's bedroom. One of her first commands as monarch was that she should have an apartment of her own.

Victoria's coronation took place on 28 June, 1838. The day began with rain; but, when she arrived at Westminster Abbey, the sun came out. Everybody agreed that it was a good sign. The ceremony was not without hitches. An ancient baron tripped over his robes as he went to pay homage. The Archbishop of Canterbury put the ring on the wrong finger; and the Bishop of Bath and Wells turned over two pages in the prayer book by mistake.

Afterwards, when Victoria returned to Buckingham Palace, she hurried upstairs. It was, she said, time to give her favourite dog its bath.

But Britain was delighted with the new Queen. After her debauched uncles, a healthy and innocent girl made a pleasant change. As one observer said, she was 'gay as a lark – like a girl on her birthday'.

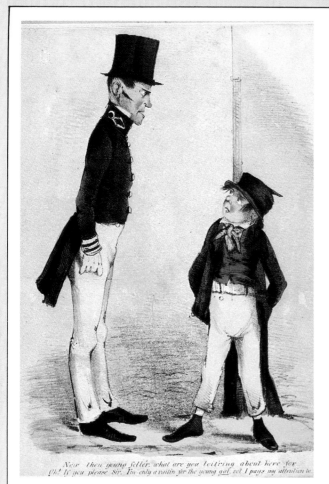

Now then young feller: what are you loitering about here for
Oh! If you please Sir, I'm only a waitin for the young gal, vot I pays my attention to.

Early policemen were called 'peelers' after their founder, Sir Robert Peel. At first, they were unpopular – not least with their young suspects.

Crime and Punishment

At the beginning of the 19th century, most people in authority believed that fear of death was the only thing that deterred would-be criminals. It was, they said, reasonable that a few should die for the good of the majority.

In 1808, a reformer named William Romilly managed to persuade the House of Commons to accept transportation for life as an alternative to hanging convicted pick-pockets. Since this crime tended to be the speciality of children, it meant that fewer youngsters would mount the gallows.

Nevertheless, in the early 19th century, there were still 220 different offences punishable by death. They ranged from big crimes such as murder and highway robbery to defacing Westminster Bridge in London, or stealing the equivalent of 25p from a shop. In the 1820s, Sir Robert Peel, the Home Secretary, introduced penal reform which reduced the number by half. But the law was still harsh. When, in 1830, a group of starving farm labourers rioted for a wage of 12½p

a day, nineteen of them were hanged – about 505 sentenced to deportation. Of this number, 481 actually sailed for Australia.

On country estates, poaching was rampant. There were gangs of villains from the cities and simple (no doubt hungry) cottage dwellers who hoped to steal some free meat. If one of the latter was captured, he was liable to a sentence of seven years transportation. But, by the time he came to court, he had possibly lost the use of a leg in one of the villainous mantraps the gentry concealed in the undergrowth (and to which the government turned a blind eye).

But reforms were slowly taking place. By 1838, murder and attempted murder were the only crimes punished by hanging. The last public execution took place in 1863, when a young man named Franz Muller was hanged for killing an old man in a railway carriage. In 1867, transportation to Australia came to an end.

At the turn of the century, riots and mob violence were still put down (often inefficiently) by the military. In the provinces, parish constables assisted by watchmen attempted to enforce law and order. In London, it was in the hands of a squad named the Bow Street Runners – which had been formed fifty years earlier by two magistrates, John and Henry Fielding.

The Bow Street Runners were underpaid. Consequently, they were prepared to accept bribes from the very villains they were supposed to arrest. This state of affairs was obviously unsatisfactory. In 1820 matters came to a head with the Cato Street Conspiracy, when ten terrorists planned to murder cabinet ministers while they sat at dinner. The plot was exposed; five assassins were hanged; the others, transported for life.

In Ireland, the Duke of Wellington had established an effective police force. When, in 1822, Sir Robert Peel became Home Secretary, the two men worked on ideas for a similar force in London. The result was that, in 1829, the Metropolitan Police was founded and its office set up in Scotland Yard. The men (known as 'peelers' or 'bobbies' after their founder) wore top hats, belted blue frock coats, and carried truncheons.

At first they were treated with hostility. But gradually the suspicion melted away and they became respected. Criminals forced out of London retreated to provincial towns – only to find that, before long, these places followed London's example. By the middle of the century, most of the urban areas in Britain had police forces, and the villains were compelled to seek bolt holes in the country.

Going to School

A 19th century reformer once remarked that a certain new building could be used equally well for a prison or a school. When Queen Victoria came to the throne, about one-third of Britain's working class children were completely uneducated. The others were having to make do with too few teachers (and many of them untrained); buildings that did, indeed, suggest the prison house; discipline that relied almost entirely on the cane or the strap; and facts that were drummed into their heads parrot fashion.

In 1833, the House of Commons had, admittedly, agreed to an annual grant to be spent on school buildings. But it was only £20,000 and it did not go very far.

As the century wore on, there were changes, and most of them were for the better. The Reform Act of 1867 made it possible for working men in towns to vote at elections. But this was ridiculous, as many of the electors could not read. Indirectly, it produced the Education Act of 1870. School boards were set up by local authorities; they could make education compulsory until the age of thirteen (previously, most pupils left at the age of twelve); and parents who could not afford to pay fees received help (but free education in all British elementary schools was not introduced until 1891).

For middle and upper class boys, there were either the fashionable public schools, such as Eton and Harrow, or grammar schools. The majority of public schools taught only Latin and Greek. There was very little discipline: bullying, drinking, and even rioting were commonplace. On the face of it, they were more likely to produce villains than intelligent gentlemen.

But here, too, reform was in the air. One of the leaders was Dr Thomas Arnold, headmaster of Rugby from 1828 until 1842. Arnold introduced mathematics, modern history and modern languages to the curriculum. No less important, he devised a system in which senior boys were given responsibility. Known as monitors (or prefects), they maintained discipline and went some way towards stamping out drinking and violence. Out of this system came organized games, which were a better way of using up youthful energy.

As time went on, many of the grammar schools began to take in boarders and became public schools – and, as the growth of industry brought more money to more people, new establishments were set up. But, as in the case of elementary schools, more attention was paid to cramming

Ragged Schools for the poor were established in the mid-19th century. Conditions were not ideal. But at least youngsters learned to read.

facts into the pupils' heads than to teaching them how to think.

Since sending boys to public schools cost a good deal of money, there was not always enough left over to pay for their sisters' educations. The popular view was that it did not very much matter. A man needed such a background to succeed in the world. Most of the professions were closed to women.

University education was more advanced in Scotland than in England, where it was still very much in the hands of the church. Oxford and Cambridge were content if they turned out clergymen and lawyers and nothing much else. Indeed, there were no science laboratories at Oxford until 1855.

Nevertheless, slow though it was, there was progress. Even the working classes could improve their store of knowledge if they attended classes at so-called Mechanics' Institutes. These establishments had originated in Scotland; but, between the 1820s and the 1830s, they spread to towns throughout industrial England. Unlike the universities, they were less concerned with teaching the classics than with passing on scientific knowledge. And this was what a century such as the 19th really needed.

Hunger

A visitor to Britain during the first half of the 19th century would no doubt have been impressed. He would have seen large factories manufacturing goods (and prosperity for their owners). He would have seen a country gradually being criss-crossed by railway lines; growing cities, and newly built houses crammed with expensive possessions.

But if he had looked beyond, he would have discovered terrible poverty. Hidden beneath the industrial landscape, there was shame. There is nothing new about unemployment: there was, indeed, plenty of it during the first part of the 19th century. Farm workers dismissed by farmers; factory hands thrown out of jobs that machines could do better; soldiers nobody wanted because there was no war for them to fight.

For many such people, the only chance of survival was the workhouse. Created by the New Poor Law of 1834, it was a terrible place, no better than a prison, and some said worse. Since men and women were not allowed in the same quarters, married couples had to be separated. The food was abominable, the labour hard. Many men were employed on breaking up stones for the road, a job little better than that given to a criminal sentenced to hard labour.

In Ireland, the poverty was fearful. In 1828, for example, the population of Cork was 117,000. Of this 60,000 were paupers – 20,000 did not even possess beds.

The Irishman's diet depended on potatoes. If the crop was good, he had just enough to eat; if not . . . In 1845, the Great Famine began. In one week the entire harvest was wiped out by a blight, which in no time crossed the sea to the lowlands of Scotland and moved north until it reached the Orkneys. During this and the next year, 700,000 people died, either from starvation, or from disease brought on by it.

In the Highlands of Scotland, the small farmers (crofters) faced another peril: sheep. Sheep farmers were prepared to pay a landlord more money for his land than an impoverished crofter could afford. What was more, they paid punctually. People were swept off the land by a tide of animals; nobody wanted them. Like the unemployed and the starving, they were thrown on the human scrap heap.

For all these people, there was only one answer to their troubles: to emigrate. The United States, Canada, Australia and other places overseas, seemed to be lands of opportunity. Here, surely, there would be a place for the unwanted men and women of Britain.

The story of the emigration trade is another scandal. At the ports of embarkation the unfortunate travellers were robbed by villainous travel agents. The ships compared unfavourably with those that used to ply the slave trade (at least the latter's captains had a financial interest in landing their cargoes alive at the journey's end). Even in such places as New York the grim trade of stripping people of their pitifully few possessions flourished.

But many never reached the other side of the Atlantic. Typhus, spread by lice, caused many to die on the voyage. The vessels became known as 'fever ships'. When a quarantine station was established on Grosse Isle at the approaches to Quebec, it was soon nick-named 'Death Isle'. And no wonder. On one day in May, 1847, there were 856 cases of typhus and cholera in the island's hospital – 470 on the ships waiting to disembark. And the patients were dying at the rate of eleven a day.

This was a fine time to live in Britain – if you were rich, if you had a job, if you were wanted. If not (as some professed) it was better to be in gaol.

English landlords who cared nothing for their tenants' poverty, and starvation when the potato crop failed, caused countless Irish families to emigrate to America.

The Great Exhibition, held in Hyde Park, London, in 1851, was Prince Albert's masterpiece. His wife, Queen Victoria, visited it no fewer than 34 times. The hall of glass in which it took place was known as the Crystal Palace.

The Great Exhibition

In February, 1840, Queen Victoria married Prince Albert of Saxe-Coburg-Gotha. She had known Albert since they were both children. By the time of their wedding in the Chapel Royal at Windsor, she was deeply in love with him.

Albert was a very serious young man. He believed in duty, industry, morality and the importance of home life. But, above all things, he delighted in technical progress.

In 1850, Albert had an idea for a great exhibition, which would show Britain's industrial skill to the world – and give the world an opportunity to demonstrate its achievements to Britain. He himself chose the site in London's Hyde Park. Two hundred and forty-three plans for the building were considered. Eventually the idea of a gardener and conservatory designer named Joseph Paxton was accepted. This great display of the world's inventions was to be housed *in a crystal palace*.

By 1 May, 1851, everything was ready. Queen Victoria performed the opening ceremony. During the next 140 days, over six million people attended. But not everyone believed that the glass roof was safe. For this reason, Victoria was the only crowned head among the visitors; the others dared not attend.

For the first three weeks, an entrance fee of 25p was charged. After that; 5p except on Fridays and Saturdays, when it went up to 12½p. It was on the 5p days that large parties of sightseers from all over the country, brought to London in excursion trains, came to this glass-cased wonderland.

A firm named Schweppes carried out the catering. Between May and October (when the exhibition closed), they served over one million bath buns, 32,000 quarts of cream, thirty-three tons of ham, and goodness knows how many soft drinks. Alcoholic beverages were not available.

When it was all over, the Crystal Palace was dismantled and presently re-erected on a site at Sydenham in South London. The profits (over £180,000) were, on the Prince's insistence, spent on educational projects. These were the forerunners of the Science Museum, the Victoria and Albert Museum, and so on, in South Kensington.

The Great Exhibition of 1851 was a timely celebration. So much had already been invented. And so much more was to come.

The Crimean War 1854-56

RUSSIA

CRIMEA
Sevastopol
Balaclava

BLACK SEA

Sinope

Constantinople
Scutari

OTTOMAN EMPIRE

GREECE

CYPRUS

Chaos in the Crimea

Soldiers in the 19th century were not expected to think. Had those who fought in the Crimean War done so, they might have wondered why they were being exposed to so much danger and hardship. What was the point of it all?

Nicholas I, Tsar of Russia, had likened the Ottoman Empire of Turkey to 'a very sick man'. Russia had occupied Turkish governed provinces on the Danube, and her fleet had wiped out a Turkish flotilla off Sinope in the Black Sea. This suggested that the next move might be the Russian occupation of Constantinople (now Istanbul) – an event that would upset the British command over the Mediterranean.

No doubt the balance of power was the cause of the war, though this argument was soon to fall flat on its face. At Austria's urging, Russia had withdrawn her forces from the Danube some while before the war broke out. Probably, like so many other conflicts, the war happened because nobody could stop it.

The object of the allies (Britain, France and Turkey) was simply to destroy the Russian naval stronghold at Sebastopol. Nobody expected the campaign to last longer than a month or two, which may have been why the British forces were so appallingly ill-prepared. In fact, Sebastopol turned out to be a much tougher nut to crack; and Russia threw things into confusion early on by attacking the British base at Balaclava.

General Colin Campbell and his 'thin red line' of Highlanders repulsed the Russians, but this success was followed by an almighty blunder.

The Earl of Cardigan should have been ordered to bring the Light Brigade into action and prevent the Russians from removing some guns from no-man's land. Unfortunately, on its way, somebody got the message wrong. The result was that Cardigan and his horse soldiers charged the wrong position. Far from being taken to the rear, these artillery pieces were manned and ready to fire. What was more, they were well supported by infantry. By the end of the luckless charge, 113 of the 673 men who took part had been killed; 134 wounded. The Russian casualties must have been very small indeed.

The men in the Crimea were short of almost everything – and especially of medical supplies and nursing staff. Since, in addition to those injured in battle, a great many were sick with cholera, the crisis was serious. The conditions in the hospital at Scutari, were unbelievably awful.

Relief came when, in November 1854, a trained nurse named Florence Nightingale arrived with a team of assistants. Miss Nightingale worked and bullied and raged and argued until she had sorted out the mess. To the wounded men and the public in Britain, she was a heroine. The high command in the Crimea, who suffered from the lash of her tongue, liked her less.

Eventually, in 1855, Sebastopol fell. The allies departed and the war was over. But the rumblings of hostilities continued until 1878, when Prime Minister Benjamin Disraeli signed the Treaty of Berlin. He brought back, he said, 'peace with honour'. More to the point, he also brought back possession of the Mediterranean island of Cyprus.

The disaster of Balaclava was the Light Brigade's charge; the triumph, the holding of the thin red line. Although (above right) Balaclava harbour was thick with ships, there were few comforts for the troops. Even the courageous Coldstream Guards (right) could not fight the unseen enemy – cholera.

Innovations
Apart from providing the army with a proper medical service, the Crimean war saw two new things. One was the Victoria Cross, which was instituted as the supreme award for valour. The other was that, for the first time, a war was reported for newspapers by professional correspondents. The first of the many was William Howard Russell of The Times. *Since he told readers in Britain how badly the campaign was being managed, he – like Miss Nightingale (above) – made the high command angry.*

The rising of the Indian sepoys against their British officers in 1857 marked the end of the East India Company's rule. Many Britons were massacred.

Mutiny in India

During Queen Victoria's reign, the British Empire stretched from the West Indies to the Far East, from Canada to South Africa. Of all these possessions, the jewel in the crown (or so it was said) was India. Strangely enough, this precious sub-continent was ruled not by the Queen nor by her government, but by businessmen with offices in the City of London. These men were directors of the East India Company – which had its own army, its own officials, its own traditions.

The object of the Company (like that of any other) was to make money. Its officials paid little heed to Indian beliefs and customs. The fact that the Indians were either Muslims or Hindus merely served to show that they were savages. To put matters right, missionaries were imported. Their aim was to convert these unbelievers to the Christian faith.

Nobody seemed to realize how bitter the resentment was. Even Indian soldiers (sepoys) serving in the Company's armies feared the missionaries. These men were sincere in their own beliefs; they were afraid of being converted by force. To make matters worse, their allowances had recently been cut. They were now in a bad mood: half afraid, half angry, and ready to listen to rumours.

The last straw came in May, 1857, when the sepoys were issued with cartridges for their new Lee Enfield rifles. They were greased with a mixture of cow and pig fat. The Hindus regarded anything to do with cows as blasphemous; the Muslims abominated pigs. Neither would handle the new ammunition – especially since, according to the latest crop of rumours, this was yet another measure to compel them to become Christians.

On 10 May, the Indian Mutiny began on the parade ground at Meerhut, a small town about fifty miles from Delhi. The sepoys were ordered to practice using the new cartridges. They refused. When the British colonel repeated the order, they turned on their officers, killing several of them.

From this moment, the mutiny spread rapidly across one thousand miles of the state of Bengal. Delhi was taken by the mutineers; Cawnpore fell; and the white population of Lucknow endured a siege lasting 140 days.

Entire European communities – women and children as well as men – were wiped out. Many fearful atrocities were committed and reinforcements had to be sent out from England before, eventually, the rising was put down.

Afterwards, there was no mercy. Mutineers were executed by the score, usually without trial. British officers (many of them easy-going, amiable, men) had been worked up into a state of fury. They committed atrocities that were just as bad as those of the rebels.

Peace was proclaimed on 8 July, 1858. In August of that year, the India Act was passed. The government of India was taken away from the Company and assumed by the Crown. A Viceroy replaced the Governor General, and the Company's troops were absorbed into the Indian Army.

The Widowed Queen

When Queen Victoria came to the throne, she had been a light hearted girl. She had enjoyed going for long rides with her first Prime Minister, Lord Melbourne. In the evenings, she had liked to dance and to play games. Her marriage to Prince Albert changed her. Under his influence, she took a much more serious view of life, and she was a strict mother to their nine children. The eldest, Princess Victoria, became the mother of Kaiser William II of Germany. The second, Edward, was to become Edward VII.

As Queen of Britain, Victoria was head of state. Nevertheless, she made it quite clear that Prince Albert was head of the family. Indeed, despite her position in life, she believed that women should remain in the background. She opposed their entry into the professions (when her daughter, Louise, went to see Dr Elizabeth Garrett – Britain's first woman doctor – she begged her host 'not to tell mama' of her visit).

'We women,' Queen Victoria once said, 'were not *made* for governing.' When she heard about a speech in favour of giving the vote to women, she said that the speaker 'ought to get a good whipping'.

Prince Albert had been very concerned about the living conditions of the working class. Two model homes had been erected in the grounds of the Great Exhibition. Later, he appointed a commission to investigate the sanitary arrangements of working class dwellings. He might have looked into matters nearer home. The cesspools at Windsor made such a stench that parts of the castle could not be used.

In November, 1861, Prince Albert became ill with typhoid fever. He died at 10.45 on the evening of 14 December. Queen Victoria was broken hearted. 'My life as a *happy* one is ended,' she wrote in her diary.

She now withdrew from public life. Her children began to undertake some of her duties, as she shut herself up at home, wondering what Albert would have done about this, and what he would have thought about that. Eventually, after two years of seclusion, people began to wonder what was the point of having a Queen whom nobody ever saw. One joker even dared to put up a notice outside Buckingham Palace. It announced that the premises were 'to be let or sold' due to 'the late occupant's declining business'.

At last, in March, 1864, Queen Victoria ended her silence by sending a letter to *The Times*

Prince Albert's memorial opposite the Albert Hall in Hyde Park. No expense was spared.

newspaper. Although it did not bear her name, there was no doubt about who was the author. It went some way towards explaining her conduct and certainly marked a turning point. Afterwards, she appeared in public again and was also seen to take a more active part in government.

During the latter part of her life, two Prime Ministers dominated politics: William Ewart Gladstone (whom she disliked) and Benjamin Disraeli (whom she loved). She called the latter 'Dizzy' and sent him bouquets of primroses picked by her ladies-in-waiting on the royal estate at Osborne, Isle of Wight.

But nobody could ever take the place of Albert. She erected monuments to him wherever it seemed to be suitable. There was, for example, a stone at Balmoral to mark the place where he shot his last deer; another at Windsor to commemorate his last pheasant shoot. The greatest was in Hyde Park, London, near the site of the Crystal Palace. It cost £60,000 and was designed by Sir Gilbert Scott who also built St Pancras railway station in London.

Passing the Time

The 19th century was an important time for sport. Not many new major outdoor games were invented, but existing ones were standardized with the drawing up of rules and the foundation of organizations to see that they were carried out.

Some ways of passing the time, such as watching cock-fighting, bear baiting and public executions, had been downright brutal, and appealed to the worst instincts of spectators. Round about the middle of the century, they were all made illegal. Prize fighting, in which the contestants fought without gloves and battered each other to the finish, yielded in 1867 to boxing. A set of rules was written down by the Marquis of Queensberry. One of them was that the competitors must wear gloves. Another limited the length of rounds to three minutes each.

Football had been a chaotic sport in which any number could take part. In 1846, at a meeting in Cambridge, proper rules were established, and each side limited to eleven players. Seventeen years later, the Football Association was formed. The first FA Cup final was played in 1872 at the Oval in London (now a cricket pitch) between the Royal Engineers and a team composed of ex-public school boys name the Wanderers. The Wanderers won 1–0.

In 1882, the cup was won by the Old Etonians, and it was not until the end of the century that professional players began to appear. But, by this time, there was another kind of football. As its name suggests, it was first played at Rugby School. The story goes that a boy named William Webb Ellis suddenly picked up the ball during a soccer game and ran with it. It may have been breaking the rules, but it seemed to be a good idea and a new sport was born.

According to some accounts, cricket of a kind had been played in Anglo-Saxon days. The first county match had taken place in 1719, when London played Kent. The Victorians wore top hats when they went out to field. In 1864 the game was brought closer to today's version, when overarm bowling replaced underarm. Tennis with strung rackets was introduced to Britain during the 16th century by an Italian priest. Henry VIII was a keen player – and, by all accounts – a very good one. Originally, it was played indoors. When it was first tried out in the open, the courts were 100 metres long.

In the 1860s, however, two gentlemen introduced lawn tennis in the grounds of a house at Leamington Spa. In 1872, the first lawn tennis club in the world was set up, and the game began to become popular. Since a much smaller court was used, it could be played in a fair sized garden. By the end of the century, no well-to-do house was complete without a tennis court. The lawn itself was often used for croquet (itself a descendent of a much older game named pall mall).

With reading now a fairly commonplace accomplishment, many people spent their evenings enjoying novels. The works of Charles Dickens (who combined good stories with scathing social comment) were extremely popular. When first published, they appeared in weekly instalments. By the end of the century, Stevenson had published *Treasure Island*, and Conan Doyle's Sherlock Holmes (magnifying glass, deerstalker, pipe and all) had arrived.

In the theatre, you could revel in the works of Gilbert and Sullivan. Towards the end of the century, two Irishmen took the world of drama by storm. One was Oscar Wilde; the other, George Bernard Shaw.

The gramophone had already been invented. Radio and TV had not. Nor could you yet go to the movies, but they were working on it. On 26 June, 1896, the world's first cinema was opened in New Orleans. They called it a 'Vitascope'. But the new craze did not reach Britain until 1901, when a picture palace was opened in the London borough of Islington.

Above: For readers of the 'Strand Magazine', there were the adventures of Sherlock Holmes and his friend Dr Watson. Left: Lord's was named after its founder, Thomas Lord. The first match was played here in 1814. Right: The Harrow football team of 1867. Many Public schools were founder members of the FA. Below: A prize fight in progress in the 1820s. In 1865, the celebrated Queensberry Rules were drawn up: bare-knuckle fighting yielded to the use of gloves.

Left: The Irish wanted to rule themselves, and Prime Minister Gladstone would gladly have allowed it. But the Conservatives had other ideas.

Right: Parnell was the voice of Irish independence, but the voice broke when he became involved in a scandal.

Trouble in Ireland

There were many reasons why the Irish were unhappy for their country to remain part of the United Kingdom. Much of the land, for example, was owned by Englishmen who pocketed their rents without ever going to see the tenants. They neither knew nor cared about the plight of these luckless peasants, who lived in mortal fear – either of starvation, or else of being evicted from their hovels.

In 1798, the Irish attempted an unsuccessful rebellion. William Pitt the Younger promised that their complaints would be examined, and that restrictions making it impossible for Irish Catholics to sit in Parliament would be abolished.

If anyone hoped that this might be the start of a road leading to Home Rule, he (or she) was in for a disappointment. Having passed this pious resolution, Pitt turned his attention to the war with France. In London, if not in Dublin, the matter seemed to have been forgotten.

A note of cheer was struck in 1829, when the Catholic Emancipation Act was passed. Since Ireland was a strongly Catholic country, it seemed to have a particular importance. As a result of it, Roman Catholics could now fill any office except that of Regent, or Lord Chancellor or (which seems to have been a pity) Lord Lieutenant of Ireland.

The potato famine that began in 1845, created enormous hardship and suffering, and led to a mass migration to America. Nor did the callous attitude of landlords do anything to help. It merely intensified a hatred of English rule and made people more determined than ever to achieve independence.

Strangely enough, the foremost fighter for Irish independence during the 19th century was a Protestant. His name was Charles Stewart Parnell. In 1873, he became leader of the Home Rule Association. Two years later, he was elected to the House of Commons.

An energetic movement to force Home Rule through Parliament began. Tenants refused to pay their rents; landlords were boycotted. An organization named Moonlighters burned haystacks, damaged property, and attacked people. In 1881, matters reached a head when Parnell was arrested. Violence increased, and he was released later in the year.

But worse was to follow. In 1882, a band named the Invincibles stabbed to death two men who were walking in Dublin's Phoenix Park. One was the newly appointed chief secretary for Ireland, Lord Frederick Cavendish; the other was the permanent under-secretary, Thomas Burke.

As a result of this double murder, the Crimes Act was passed in the same year. It was now possible for people to be convicted without a trial

by jury. To make matters worse, tenants who seemed to be trouble makers could be (and were) ruthlessly turned out of their homes.

In England, your views on the Irish question depended on whether you were a Liberal or a Conservative. In 1886, the Liberal leader, Mr Gladstone, proposed an Irish Home Rule Bill. All Irish affairs were to be managed by a parliament in Dublin – except foreign policy, defence and customs and excise.

Conservative feeling against it (with which the Queen agreed) ran so high, that a general election had to take place. The Liberals were thrown out, and home rule was forgotten – except in Ireland where there were more outbreaks of violence.

Parnell was still the leading voice of Irish independence. But, by 1890, he was in trouble. He had become involved in a scandal in which a certain Captain O'Shea divorced his wife and named him as co-respondent. He was advised to resign from his leadership of the Irish nationalists, but he refused. In the following year, he married the former Mrs O'Shea. That autumn, he died.

In 1893, Gladstone was back in power and making another attempt to win home rule. The bill was accepted by the Commons, but thrown out by the strong Conservative opposition in the House of Lords.

The century passed into history with the Irish question still unresolved.

The Great Empire

On 22 June, 1897, Queen Victoria celebrated her Diamond Jubilee. Before setting out in procession to St Paul's Cathedral, she went into the telegraph room at Buckingham Palace. She pressed an electric button. Within seconds, a message was being transmitted to every corner of her Empire. It read: 'From my heart I thank my people. May God bless them'.

This was the largest Empire ever known. The Union Jack flew over lands covering nearly a quarter of the earth's surface, and was saluted by nearly a quarter of the world's population. Its influence ranged from remote islands in the West Indies, to territories in China; from a great deal of Africa to all of India; to Australia, Canada and New Zealand – with Burma and part of New Guinea thrown in for good measure.

Since the Mutiny, Indian affairs had been taken over by the Government. In 1876, on Disraeli's advice, Queen Victoria had proclaimed herself Empress of India, and she undoubtedly regarded this great sub-continent with particular favour. In her house at Osborne on the Isle of Wight, she had one room decorated in the Indian manner. It contained many gifts from rajahs (Indian princes).

Keeping such a large and scattered collection of possessions under control did, of course, sometimes present difficulties. At the time of the Queen's Silver Jubilee, there was trouble in Southern Africa. The Cape Colony on the tip of the continent was owned by the British. To the north of it, the Transvaal was occupied by Dutch colonists (Boers) under President Kruger.

The root of the matter dated back to 1885, when gold was discovered in the Transvaal. This caused a great many people to emigrate there in the hope of making fortunes. The newcomers were heavily taxed by President Kruger and they were not allowed to vote in elections.

Cecil Rhodes, Prime Minister of the Cape Colony, hoped that the new settlers (Uitlanders as they were called by the Boers) might rebel. If all went well, this would give him an opportunity to march in and create an entirely British South Africa. To encourage the Uitlanders, he stationed a force of about five hundred horsemen on the border. They were commanded by Dr Leander Starr Jameson. The moment signs of a revolt became apparent, Dr Jameson was to give his men orders to ride into the Transvaal.

But Jameson was impatient. When nothing happened, he decided to take matters into his

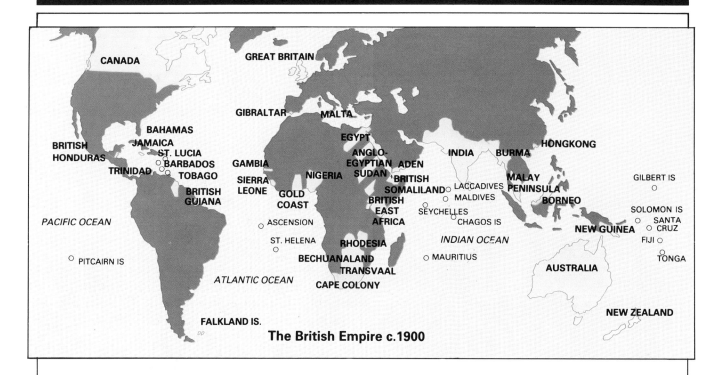

The British Empire c.1900

own hands. On 29 December, 1895, he and his mounted men crossed the border.

It was a disaster. The Uitlanders, who were negotiating with Kruger, did not require any help – indeed, the presence of Jameson and his warriors was the last thing they wanted. The result was that Jameson was captured and handed back to the British. To save their faces, they sent him to prison for fifteen months and insisted that Rhodes must resign.

To add to the trouble Kruger received a telegram of congratulations from Kaiser William II of Germany. The Boer leader became inflated by self-importance; in 1899 he attacked the British possessions of Natal and the Cape Colony. The Boer war had begun.

But, elsewhere in the Empire, there was peace. When Queen Victoria died at Osborne in 1901, one of the nicest things was said by a Zulu chief. He remarked, 'I shall see another star in the sky'.

Above: In 1900, Britain still ruled much of the world as this map shows.

Left: Queen Victoria loved India and was proud to be its Empress. But she never actually went there. At her home on the Isle of Wight, however, she played an elaborate game of 'let's pretend'.

Right: In 1885, General Gordon was besieged in Khartoum by a fanatic called the Mahdi and his followers. A relief expedition arrived too late; Gordon was killed and the soldiers turned back. Revenge came in 1898, when troops led by Kitchener crushed the rebels. But, by this time, the Mahdi was dead.

Britain
in the
Twentieth Century

*Drained by two world wars and
shorn of its empire, the story of twentieth-
century Britain is one of profound domestic
change. It includes a great rise in standards of
living for the vast majority, the creation
of the Welfare State – and the dawn
of the computer age.*

Edward VII liked to host lavish shooting parties at Sandringham. Among guests seen here in 1907 were the Kaiser of Germany, and Edward's son and daughter-in-law, the future King George V and Queen Mary.

The Edwardian Epoch

Queen Victoria's eldest son, Albert Edward, was fifty-nine when she died. His love of pleasure had shocked his straight-laced father and alarmed his mother. She once sadly remarked, 'It quite irritates me to see him in the room'. She seldom, if ever, took him into her confidence.

It may seem to have been a bad upbringing for a monarch. Nevertheless, after the Boer War ended in 1902, the years of Edward VII's reign were a period of stability.

The new king showed that he was shrewd, especially in affairs of foreign policy. In 1904, after he had visited Paris, the Entente Cordiale was established between Britain and France. Later, when Russia joined, it became the Triple Entente. In both cases, it was a declaration of friendship rather than a military alliance, though it could easily be turned into one.

On a less historic level, King Edward VII was one of the first people to undergo an operation for an appendicitis. It was carried out in a room at Buckingham Palace a few weeks before his coronation. He was the first person to have his trousers creased at the back and front (before he started the fashion as the result of a mistake by his valet, they were creased at the sides).

During his reign, there were all sorts of innovations. The first motor car to be manufactured was exhibited at the Paris World Fair in 1889. Edward had his first trip in one when visiting an exhibition in London in 1896. On 1 December, 1900, he bought the first ever royal car. It was a Daimler.

Although only the comparatively well-to-do could afford them, the craze for cars developed quickly. By the time of his death in 1910, there were many more of them in London than there were horses.

But this was by no means the only advance. In 1906, a revolutionary new battleship was completed for the Royal Navy. She was named HMS *Dreadnought*. With greater gun power and faster speed, she made everything else out-of-date. Germany, fearing war with Britain, was quick to adopt the new ideas. Soon there was a race between the two powers to build as many of these super warships as they could.

Balloons had been making journeys in the sky for some time. In 1903, the brothers Orville and Wilbur Wright in America, showed the world that powered flight was possible. The Wrights

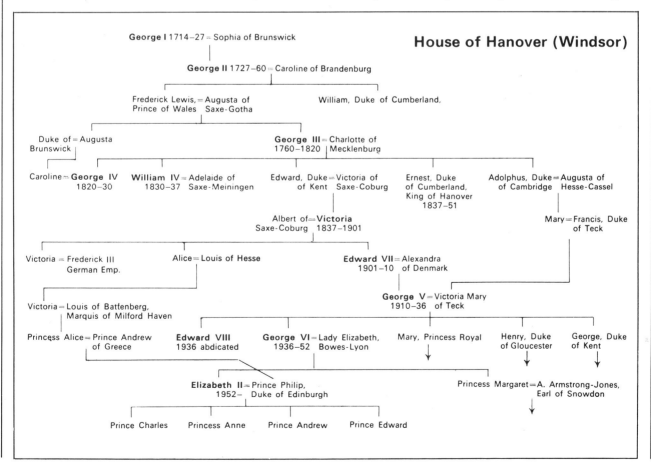

House of Hanover (Windsor)

121

took their invention to Europe, and many enthusiasts began manufacturing aeroplanes. Most of them were unreliable and often dangerous. Nevertheless, in 1909, a Frenchman named Louis Bleriot became the first man to fly across the English Channel.

Wireless had already arrived when Edward VII came to the throne. But a big step forward was made in 1901, when a message was transmitted from a station in Cornwall and received in Newfoundland.

There were, it seemed, so many new frontiers waiting to be crossed, so many new worlds of ideas to be conquered. In 1912, Captain Robert Falcon Scott, set off into the unknown by sledge in an attempt to reach the South Pole. He arrived

there in the end, only to discover that a party of Norwegians led by Roald Amundsen had got there first. It was a bitter disappointment. On their way back to their ship, the *Terra Nova*, Scott and his companions died of hunger and exposure within eleven miles of a well-stocked dump of food supplies.

But there was a tragedy on a much greater scale in May of that year. The giant liner *Titanic* – a floating luxury hotel – was on her maiden voyage to New York, when she struck an iceberg and sank. The sea was calm, but the safety measures were inadequate. Only 843 of the 2,340 people on board her survived.

In Britain, women were still not allowed to vote. Not surprisingly, many of them were angry about this. In 1903, a lady name Emmeline Pankhurst tried to put the situation right by forming the Women's Social and Political Union. During the next eleven years, Mrs Pankhurst and her members protested noisily – and often violently.

But there was much greater violence to come: something that would make votes for women, the discovery of the South Pole, and even great liners like the *Titanic*, seem insignificant. In these new circumstances, HMS *Dreadnought*, and the aeroplanes that the Wright brothers had invented, would become vitally important. The world was hurtling towards a war that would be unlike any war that had ever been fought before – and much more terrible.

In 1903, suffragettes, led by Mrs Pankhurst, began an eleven-year campaign to obtain votes for women. The police took them into custody, but the ladies were undaunted.

HMS Dreadnought, completed in 1906, was the first of a new breed of battleship, faster and more heavily armed than anything there had been before.

The Way to War

People still argue about why the First World War (often referred to as the 'Great War') broke out. The events that led up to it were as follows:-

On 28 June, 1914, the Archduke Franz Ferdinand of Austria and his wife were paying a state visit to the Bosnian town of Sarajevo (Now in Yugoslavia, but then part of the Austro-Hungarian empire). The neighbouring Serbs (also part of the empire) were anxious to become independent. As the Archduke and Duchess were being driven through the streets, the driver stopped – uncertain of which route to take. This gave a Serbian student named Gavrilo Princip his chance. Firing two shots at short range, he assassinated the royal couple.

It was entirely a matter of luck. If the car had not halted, Princip would never have succeeded. Indeed, a bomb attempt, made by another student earlier in the day, had failed.

Austria immediately issued an ultimatum to Serbia. Serbia agreed to all the points; but, nevertheless, Austrian troops crossed the frontier. One by one, all the major European powers became involved. Russia was pledged to aid Serbia. The Tsar mobilized his armies. Germany had promised to assist Austria; France was treaty-bound to come to Russia's help. As for Britain, an agreement signed in 1839 compelled the Government to support Belgium, should that country be invaded.

Kaiser William of Germany mistook Russian mobilization for an act of war. He pulled out a plan written at the turn of the century by a former Chief of the German General Staff, named Field Marshal von Schlieffen. Von Schlieffen's idea was that, to conquer Russia, France must be overrun first. In order to by-pass the defences on the frontier, the German armies should pour through Belgium, fan out, and encircle Paris.

Once the Kaiser had made up his mind to fight, everything happened very quickly. On 1 August, 1914, Germany declared war on Russia. On 3 August, she declared war on France, and invaded Belgium. On the following day, Britain declared war on Germany. The only person who was untroubled was Field Marshal von Schlieffen. He had died eight years previously.

Right: On 28 June, 1914, Archduke Franz Ferdinand, heir to the Austrian throne, visited Sarajevo with his wife where the couple were assassinated by a student named Gavrilo Princip. Princip was arrested (below) and sentenced to 20 years hard labour. He died after serving four of them.

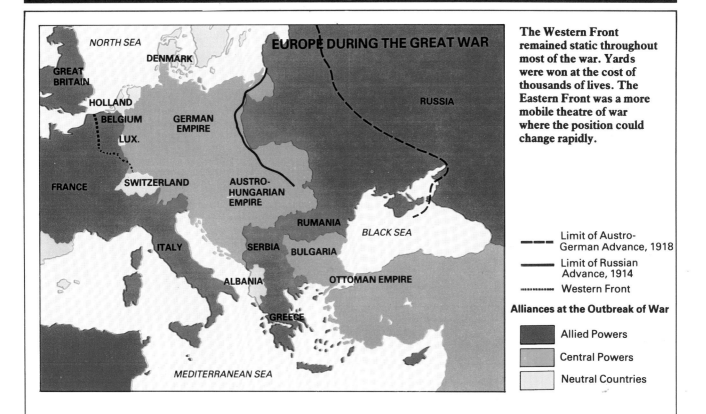

EUROPE DURING THE GREAT WAR

NORTH SEA
DENMARK
GREAT BRITAIN
HOLLAND
BELGIUM
LUX.
GERMAN EMPIRE
RUSSIA
FRANCE
SWITZERLAND
AUSTRO-HUNGARIAN EMPIRE
ITALY
SERBIA
RUMANIA
BLACK SEA
BULGARIA
ALBANIA
OTTOMAN EMPIRE
GREECE
MEDITERRANEAN SEA

The Western Front remained static throughout most of the war. Yards were won at the cost of thousands of lives. The Eastern Front was a more mobile theatre of war where the position could change rapidly.

———— Limit of Austro-German Advance, 1918

———— Limit of Russian Advance, 1914

············· Western Front

Alliances at the Outbreak of War

Allied Powers

Central Powers

Neutral Countries

The Great War

That two revolver shots, fired by a student, could unleash such a disastrous torrent of events may seem surprising. But they did. Europe was now struggling for survival in the most fearful war it had ever known. What was worse, von Schlieffen's theory was wrong. It was not necessary to overrun France to beat Russia. At the battle of Tannenberg (26–28 August, 1914) one of Russia's two armies was wiped out; 90,000 of her troops were taken prisoner and a great many killed and wounded. Her military strength had been greatly exaggerated.

At first, most people believed that the war would be over quickly. The trouble was that the opposing armies in France became deadlocked. They dug themselves in, occupying mile upon mile of trenches, with a stretch of muddy, shell-battered no-man's land in between. To attempt an attack over this open ground was madness. But the generals attempted it, and the soldiers died.

The casualties were beyond belief. Between July and November, 1916, there was heavy fighting along the line of the River Somme. During the first day of the attack by the Allies, 20,000 British troops were killed. When, at last, it ended, 420,000 British soldiers lay dead: 20,000 French, and about 450,000 Germans.

At first, the generals tried to make excuses for their failures. For example, the Battle of Neuve Chapelle (March, 1915) did nothing whatever for the British cause. Afterwards, the commander-in-chief, Sir John French, complained that he had not received enough shells. The government put the blame on munition workers; accused them of spending too much time in public houses and not enough in their factories. The result was that a Bill was passed in the House of Commons – insisting that the pubs be closed in the afternoons.

Everything that anyone could think of was done in an attempt to break the deadlock. Turkey came into the war on Germany's side in December, 1914. The First Lord of the Admiralty, Winston Churchill, proposed the sending of warships to the Dardanelles. It would, he said, create a diversion – as well as opening up a supply route to Russia. The Navy, he insisted, could handle it on its own. This turned out to be impossible. In February 1915, troops were landed, but they fared no better. Eventually the whole attempt was abandoned.

On the Western Front, the search was on for a new weapon that might overcome the snags of trench warfare. In the second battle of Ypres (April 1915), the Germans used poison gas for the first time. It produced fearful suffering. But it did not affect the course of the war.

On the Somme and, later, in the Battle of

Cambrai (November, 1917) the British used tanks. The very sight of them created panic in the enemy ranks. But, since the generals did not know how to use them, they were not very effective. For one thing, like cavalry, they needed to be supported by infantry (which they were not – the foot soldiers could not keep up with them).

Nothing, it seemed, went as anyone had

Ireland

Anyone who read the newspapers during the days immediately before the outbreak of World War I might have imagined that Ireland was a more likely source of fighting than Europe. Although a Bill, promising Home Rule, had been introduced in 1912, it had never been passed. It was not until May, 1914, that Parliament finally gave it approval. Nor was the situation made easier by a sizeable minority of Irishmen living in Ulster – who opposed independence.

In 1913, a man named James Connolly had formed the Irish Citizens Army to drive the British out. On Easter Sunday, 1916, a rising broke out in Dublin. For five days, a small force held out in the City's main post office. Eventually the leaders – Connolly, Eoin MacNeill and Patrick Pearse – were captured and executed by firing squad. The revolt fizzled out. Later, a few thousand Irishmen were sent without trial to concentration camps in England.

'Flu

The guns of the combined armies killed 9,700,000 people in World War I, and it took them more than four years. Towards the end of it, a germ named Spanish 'Flu accounted for 21,600,000 lives (237,000 in Great Britain alone) – and did it in six months. The bug, which originated in Spain, did much of its damage because people were weakened by the stress of war and badly under-nourished. Since this was many years before the discovery of penicillin, pneumonia often came in its wake. It was this that caused the deaths.

Top left: General Kitchener needed a million men. He asked for them personally – on this now famous poster.

Below: The aftermath of the Third Battle of Ypres, 1917, shows the total devastation caused by the First World War.

expected. Using Zeppelin airships, the Germans hoped to create fear and destruction in British towns and cities. In April, 1915, London suffered its first air attack. But these great airships were an easy prey for the British anti-aircraft guns and fighter aircraft. By the late spring of 1917, the Zeppelin raids had petered out.

At sea, the admirals imagined that the big battle would be fought between the large surface fleets – somewhat along the lines of Trafalgar. There was just such an engagement when the German High Seas Fleet and the British Grand Fleet clashed in the vicinity of Jutland on 31 May, 1916. There were severe casualties and a dozen ships were sunk (six German and six British), but there was no outright victory.

More significant was a very different kind of naval warfare, fought from beneath the ocean's surface by submarines. Between 1914 and 1918, 14,820,000 tons of shipping were sunk by Ger-man U-boats and Britain was very nearly starved to death. It was, indeed, use of U-boat warfare against merchant ships – beginning with the sinking of the Cunarder RMS *Lusitania* on 17 May, 1915 – that brought the United States into the war on 6 April, 1917.

When, on 8 August, 1918, the Allied armies began a counter-attack on the Western Front, there were half a million Americans to strengthen the thrust. It became too much for the Germans. On 11 November of that year, the German high command signed an armistice agreement in a railway restaurant car that had been parked for the purpose in a forest clearing near the French town of Compiegne.

At about the same time, Kaiser William was hurrying by car to Holland and exile. The war had cost three-quarters of a million British lives. Whether it had achieved anything was, perhaps, doubtful.

Above: The engines of war took to the air. Aeroplanes and airships were used for bombing and reconnaissance. The navy, now, had eyes in the sky. Left: The army depended on shells. With the men fighting at the front, much of the factory labour force was composed of women.

Left: The cinema had arrived, and one of the favourites was the comedian Buster Keaton, seen here in *The General*. Below: In the General Strike of 1926 the Government feared riots, and armoured cars patrolled the streets.

Life in the 'Twenties

During World War I, the people of Britain were promised that this was 'the war to end war', and that it would build 'a land fit for heroes'. Afterwards, many of them must have laughed bitterly. Far from ending war, the peace treaty almost made certain that, sooner or later, there would be another conflict in Europe. As for the 'land of heroes', Britain in post-war years was nothing of the kind.

In 1918, as a kind of reward for good behaviour, the Representation of the People Act gave the vote to all men over twenty-one years of age; to all women over thirty. But that was as far as the Government's generosity went. There were not enough jobs for ex-servicemen; and, in 1921, the unemployment figure reached two million.

The revolution in Russia had shown what happened when a dissatisfied working class found strong leaders. In Britain, matters reached a head in May, 1926, when a strike by coal miners (protesting against cuts in pay) sparked off a General Strike. All workers in heavy industry supported the miners – plus those in a good many other trades. Volunteers protected by police drove trains, lorries and buses; gas and electricity supplies were restricted.

At first, there were fears that riots – or even civil war – might break out. But there was nothing worse than an occasional scuffle, and the strike turned out to be a nine-days' wonder. The miners held out for longer. Eventually, they had to surrender and return to work longer hours for less money.

Next year, a law making general strikes illegal was passed. It survived until 1946.

But this was the gloomy side of life. In 1919, two Englishmen, John Alcock and Arthur Whit-ten Brown, took off from a field in Newfoundland and, flying an adapted Vickers Vimy bomber, became the first to fly the Atlantic non-stop.

On land, the world speed record was broken and broken again. In 1927, a driver named Henry Segrave crossed the 200 mph mark with a speed of 203.79 mph. Less than a year later, Malcolm Campbell capped it with 206.96 mph – and so the friendly rivalry went on until Segrave was killed on Lake Windermere in 1930. He was trying to beat the world water speed record at the time.

The cinema had arrived and there were picture houses all over the country. At first the films were silent, accompanied by a pianist or (in the large cinemas) by an orchestra. But, in 1927, a film named *The Jazz Singer* changed all that. It was the first talking picture.

Wireless sets were now to be found in many homes. In 1922, an organization named the British Broadcasting Company was formed to transmit programmes. In 1927, its name was changed to the British Broadcasting Corporation. It came under the Post Office: to use a receiver, you had to buy a licence. The BBC did not, like radio in most other countries, rely on advertising for its money.

There were big bands. The night clubs of London were packed. Everyone was having a marvellous time – except those who were out of work, and those who realized that peace could not last for ever. Before long, Europe would be in trouble once more.

The economic depression of the thirties led to massive
unemployment and demonstrations such as the famous
march from Jarrow to London in 1936 (above). But the
rich remained rich and could afford to keep up with
fashion (left). In Germany, the rise of Adolf Hitler (below)
coincided with economic recovery, and many Germans
mistook him for a saviour.

The Nervous 'Thirties

Three things loomed over the 1930s in a way that
made almost everything else seem unimportant.
They were: the economic depression, the abdication of a king, and the fear of war.

The depression began in America, where
prices on the stock market suddenly slumped.
Fortunes were wiped out overnight; even mil-
lionaires were among those who committed
suicide rather than face financial ruin. Like a
disease, the economic disaster was blown across
the Atlantic, where it reached Britain in 1930. In
1929, a Labour Government under Ramsay Macdonald had come to power. Mr Macdonald and
his ministers grappled with the crisis – and
failed. Two years afterwards (in 1931), the
Cabinet was replaced by a national coalition (a
government made up from people of all parties).

Unemployment figures reached new heights,
especially in the industrial north and in South
Wales. On every street corner, there were groups
of jobless men, who looked hungry, sad, and
sometimes defeated. In Jarrow, to mention only
one town, two-thirds of the population were
permanently unemployed.

On 20 January, 1936, King George V died. His
son Edward, the popular Prince of Wales,
became King Edward VIII. But, ever since 1932,

he had been living a secret life. In that year he fell in love with Mrs Wallis Simpson – an American divorcee who was now married to her second husband.

As head of the Church of England, the British sovereign cannot be involved with divorce. Eventually, King Edward would have to make up his mind. He would either have to end his association with Mrs Simpson, or else give up the throne. He did not seem inclined to do either. In October, 1936, Wallis Simpson quietly divorced Mr Simpson, and the King made it clear that he intended to marry her. This was impossible; a twice divorced woman could never be Queen of England.

In early December, Edward made his decision. If the choice really had to be between the crown and his loved one, he would choose the latter. On the evening of 10 December, he made a farewell broadcast to the British people. Afterwards, he crossed to France in a destroyer – to spend the rest of his life in exile.

George VI became king. Edward VIII, after a short reign in which he was never crowned, married Wallis Simpson on 26 June, 1937.

In 1919, the Treaty of Versailles – which concluded the peace making after World War I – had imposed extremely harsh terms on Germany. Unemployment over there was far, far worse than in Britain. Governments came and went; inflation reached such peaks that money became worthless.

In 1933, a former corporal in the German army, Adolf Hitler, was elected Chancellor. By what seemed to be a miracle, he jerked Germany out of its economic chaos and set himself up as dictator. Almost immediately, he renounced the Treaty of Versailles. He pledged himself to win back all the lands that had been taken away. In 1936, German troops re-occupied the Rhineland. In 1938, he annexed Austria; later in the year his soldiers invaded Czechoslovakia. Poland was next on his list.

Throughout this period, when military action would have halted the German march, the British and French governments looked on as if in a daze. The British Prime Minister, Neville Chamberlain, visited Hitler at the time of the Czech crisis in 1938. When he returned, he happily announced that he had achieved 'peace in our time'.

Hitler knew otherwise. At the beginning of September, 1939, German tanks rumbled across the frontier into Poland. This time, there could be no more peacemaking. The Second World War had begun.

The Second World War

Posters such as this one illustrated Britain's fear of a German invasion, and people were warned to report anything out of the ordinary.

The First World War happened as if by accident. The second did not. Hitler was head of the National Socialist (Nazi) Party in Germany. From the moment he came to power, freedom was abolished. Newspapers, films and radio were censored by the Minister of Propoganda, Dr Josef Goebbels. Anyone who dared to disagree with the government was removed to a concentration camp.

Jews, especially, were persecuted. The extent of the brutality did not become clear until after the war. Then it was discovered that something like six million had died in these hideous prison camps.

Although the conflict of 1914–18 is known as 'the First *World* War', the conflict was mostly confined to Europe. Apart from the United States and countries within the British Empire, the nations involved were European. The fighting that went on from 1939 until 1945 really *was* a world war. All the world's oceans saw naval combat. On land, battles were fought in the frozen north of Norway and on the scorching sands of the North African desert; at places as far apart as the shores of the English Channel and the jungles of Burma.

Germany invaded Poland and overran it in less than three weeks. After that, there was a lull (people called it 'the phoney war') until the following spring. Then, as if trying to make up for lost time, events moved quickly.

On 9 April, 1940, German forces invaded Norway and Denmark. One month later, Hitler's armies overran Holland and Belgium; advanced into France. They called it the *blitzkrieg* (lightning war). Back at Cambrai in 1917, the generals had not known how to employ tanks. This time, the Germans were using them, and they handled them as tanks should be handled. Columns of steel swept across the countryside, smashing opposition as they went.

By 29 May, a large part of the British army was trapped on the French coast at Dunkirk – surrounded on three sides by German armour. During the next five days, a fleet made up of pretty well everything that could float (including yachts and paddle steamers) went to the aid of the stranded soldiers and brought them back to England.

On 22 June, France surrendered. The dining car in which the 1918 armistice terms were signed had been preserved in Paris. Hitler now insisted that it be brought to the forest clearing near Compiegne. It was here that Marshal Petain, now the French leader, signed away his country's freedom. The score, at last, was even.

The next step should have been the German invasion of Britain. Hitler had a plan for it; he named it 'Operation Sea Lion'. But, before it could be carried out, the RAF had to be shot from the skies. Throughout August and into September, the Luftwaffe (German air force) attacked British aerodromes. As Winston Churchill, who had become Prime Minister on 10 May, said 'The Battle of France is over. I expect the Battle of Britain is about to begin'.

But the RAF not only survived; it inflicted severe losses on the Luftwaffe. Soon Hitler realised that Operation Sea Lion could not take place. He ordered his aircraft to bomb British cities instead. The Battle of Britain gave way to what people called the 'Blitz'.

There were few civilian casualties in World War I. It was fought by soldiers against other soldiers. The second World War involved everybody. Food, petrol, even clothes were rationed. People were conscripted into industry as well as into the armed forces. And, in the air raids, a

great many civilians died.

On 10 June, Mussolini – the dictator of Italy and Hitler's friend – had declared war on Britian. In those days, Italy had important colonies in Libya. The fighting switched to the North African desert. When Hitler saw that Italian soldiers were surrendering by the thousand, he sent the Afrika Korps under one of his most brilliant generals, Erwin Rommel, to their aid. By the middle of 1941, much of the Mediterranean was in German and Italian hands – though the Royal Navy, despite heavy losses, managed to keep the sea lanes open.

But other things were about to happen. Part of Hitler's dream was to conquer Russia and to turn it into a land of slaves. On 22 June, 1941, the invasion began. By 16 October, German troops were within sixty miles of Moscow. Perhaps the German leader (they called him the 'Fuehrer') should have studied the misfortunes of Napoleon more carefully. He, too, had hoped to invade England and failed; he, too, had come close to overwhelming Russia – and failed.

The war was spreading. On 7 December, 1941, the Japanese fleet came within air-strike distance of the American island of Hawaii in the Pacific. Its warplanes took off from the carriers, and launched a sudden and completely unexpected attack on the United States naval base at Pearl Harbor.

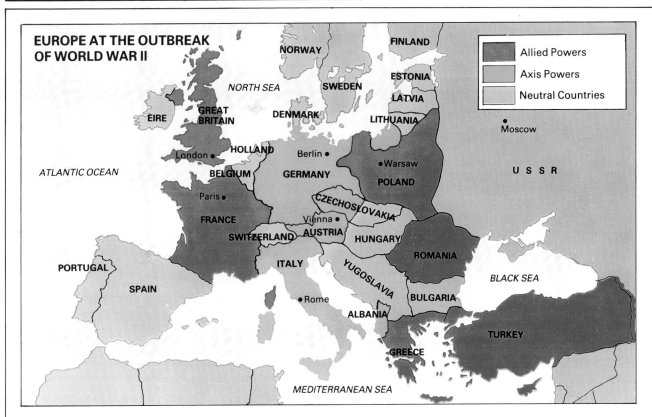

EUROPE AT THE OUTBREAK OF WORLD WAR II

■	Allied Powers
■	Axis Powers
□	Neutral Countries

Left: Winston Churchill. Described as 'the greatest Englishman', he brought the nation through defeat and gave it victory.

Above: The map shows Britain and her allies – Germany and hers. The USA joined the former in 1941, after the attack on Pearl Harbor.

Below: On 6 June, 1944, Allied soldiers landed on Normandy beaches. The liberation of Europe had begun.

The date: 7 December, 1941. Japanese carrier aircraft devastated the US fleet at Pearl Harbor

Next day, America and Britain declared war on Japan. By the time 1942 was over, Hong Kong, Singapore, and the Dutch East Indies were all in Japanese hands. The outlook was dismal.

But in North Africa and Europe, the tide of fortune was gradually changing in the Allies' favour. The brunt of the fighting in North Africa had been in the hands of the British 8th Army. Faced by Rommel's Afrika Korps, they had been driven back until it had seemed possible that the Germans might reach Cairo. But the retreat came to an end at a point (it was too small to, call a town) on the Egyptian frontier. It was named El Alamein.

In August, 1942, command of the 8th Army had been taken over by a general named Montgomery. In October of that year, he ordered his men to attack. By 4 November, Rommel and his men were in full retreat. At the year's end, a force of British and American troops landed in Algeria and marched eastwards. The Afrika Korps was now crushed between two armies.

It was not, Churchill told the British people, 'the beginning of the end; but the end of the beginning'.

When 1943 came to an end, the Germans had been driven out of North Africa, and British and American soldiers were advancing northwards up Italy from Sicily. On 4 June, 1944, the 5th Army entered Rome.

For some while, the supreme Allied commander, General Dwight Eisenhower, had been planning an invasion of France. On 6 June, 1944, despite unfavourable weather, D-Day (as it was called) began. The forces landed on Normandy beaches and fought their way inland. On the Eastern front, the Russians were attacking heavily. It would surely not be long before the war ended.

Hitler – as a last, desperate, measure – launched an offensive in the Ardennes district of Belgium. There was very heavy fighting over Christmas and for some days afterwards. The Germans were helped by bad weather, which kept the Allied aircraft on the ground. But then the skies cleared; the fighters and bombers took off, and the German attack ground to a halt.

Air raids over Britain by conventional bombers were a thing of the past (unlike the situation in Germany, when formations of a thousand or more aircraft were pounding cities to the ground – day and night). In the latter part of 1944, however, new weapons menaced London. Known as the VI and V2, these were flying bombs which did not require pilots. The RAF managed to shoot down a good many VIs. The V2s were harder to combat. But nothing, now, could help Germany. The Russians were converging on Berlin; the British and Americans were moving eastwards across the country. On 30 April, 1945, Hitler committed suicide in his Berlin headquarters. On 8 May, the war in Europe came to an end.

In the Far East, things had not been going at all well for the Japanese. Nevertheless, they might have kept the war going for a good deal longer if, on 6 August, the Americans had not dropped an atomic bomb on Hiroshima. Three days later, they unleashed another over Nagasaki. On 14 August Japan surrendered.

These were the first (and, so far – thankfully – the only) occasions on which a nuclear weapon has been used in warfare. They demonstrated a terrifying power of destruction, and science has since made them even more devastating. Peace had come at last; but, with it, fear of mankind's ability to destroy the world.

On 6 August, 1945, the atomic bomb was used for the first time – on Hiroshima in Japan. More than 80,000 people died. War had achieved yet another horror.

It rained for most of the day, but this did not spoil the splendour of Queen Elizabeth II's coronation on 2 June, 1953. Afterwards, the royal family appeared in the balcony of Buckingham Palace. The crowd cheered – and went on cheering.

Peace and Welfare

The survivors of the First World War may have felt that they were the victims of a confidence trick. Life afterwards was certainly no better than it had been before. The warriors who took part in the second were determined that history should not repeat itself. This time, things were definitely going to be different – and better.

Ever since Churchill came to power in 1940, the country had been governed by a coalition. On 5 July, 1945, largely on the insistence of the Labour Party, the nation went to the polls. The result surprised a good many people. Churchill (a Conservative) had shown himself to be an excellent leader in wartime. But now, with the prospect of peace ahead, the nation declared itself in favour of a Labour government headed by Clement Attlee.

The scales had been turned by the large number of servicemen who voted. They did not wish to return to 'the bad old days'. Labour, they believed, was more likely to produce a change. And there were changes – many of them. Ever since 1941, a civil servant named W.H. Beveridge had been working on a plan to protect people against hardship. It was based on a system of national insurance. From it grew the so-called Welfare State, and its great innovation the National Health Service, introduced in 1948.

The coal mines and the railways were nationalized, which means that their ownership was taken over by the state. Nobody minded much. The railways were almost bankrupt and the management of the pits had not been good. When it came to other industries, however, there was more controversy. For instance, steel was nationalized by one government (Labour), de-nationalized by another (Conservative), and re-nationalized by a third (Labour).

Overseas, the British Empire was breaking up.

In 1947, Earl Mountbatten was appointed Viceroy of India. His task was to haul down the Union Jack and hand the country over to the Indians. But things were not to be so simple. India was divided into Hindus and Moslems – each with an entirely different religion and customs, and each opposed to the other. As a result, the sub-continent had to be partitioned – with India for the Hindus and Pakistan for the Moslems.

During the next decade and beyond, the nation's former colonies went the way of India, until the British Empire was wiped off the map.

The war was over. Peace had come, but certainly not prosperity. Britain was up to its ears in debt to America. Rationing had to be continued; the shelves in many shops were still empty. There was not enough money to import the luxuries we have today.

By 1951, however, the economic situation was improving. Since this was the centenary of the Great Exhibition, there might be an excuse for a celebration. The result was the Festival of Britain. Exhibitions showing British achievements in art, science, and industry, were mounted on the South Bank of the River Thames in London and throughout the country. There were pageants, festivals and a lot of fun. At first, the press mocked it, and the Government was accused of wasting money. But it was undoubtedly one of the most magnificent displays the country has ever seen. People, tired of austerity, loved it.

In 1952, King George VI died, and the present Queen came to the throne. Her reign was heralded as the beginning of a 'new Elizabethan era', and things certainly seemed to be looking up. Four years later, the Conservative Prime Minister, Harold Macmillan, was able to say 'Most people have never had it so good'. It may have been a political boast, but it happened to be true.

133

Above: The ill-fated Comet heralded the jet age of civil aviation.

Left: To begin with, they were just ordinary Liverpool lads with a gift for music. But soon they were to bring a new sound to Britain.

Right: On 29 May, 1953, Edmund Hillary and Sherpa Tenzing (shown here) conquered Everest. The triumph made big newspaper headlines on Coronation Day.

The Changing World

The scientists and engineers opened the door to a new world. During the 1950s and 1960s, at least three important revolutions occurred: in travel, entertainment and power. And yet, strangely enough, all of them owed their origins to the war years before.

As early as 1940, there had been plans to produce jet-powered aircraft in Britain, and in 1941 one of these machines was actually flown. By the end of 1944, Vampire and Meteor jet fighter aeroplanes were being manufactured. So far as combat planes were concerned, the piston engine was obsolete.

One of the few good things about war is that it speeds up technical progress. Inventions devised to win battles find their way into civilian life, and so it was with the jet engine. In 1946, the de Havilland Aircraft Corporation began work on a jet-powered airliner. It was to be called the Comet.

On 2 May, 1952, the first Comet in commercial service took off from London to South Africa. Unhappily, its fuselage contained a serious design flaw, which was to cause two fatal crashes and to hold up development. Nevertheless, in October, 1958 Comet IV began regular flights across the Atlantic to New York. The effect was dramatic. The time for the crossing was cut by half, more passengers could be carried, and the aircraft flew at altitudes where the weather was calm.

Suddenly, the century-long era of giant passenger liners was over. A new age of travel – leading to such pleasures as the package tour holiday overseas – became possible.

Television had been invented by John Logie Baird in 1926. By the outbreak of World War II, the BBC was running a transmitting station at the Alexandra Palace in North London, and some (though not very many) families owned sets.

War put a stop to everything (though the cathode ray tube, which is the heart of a TV set, played an important part in radar). In 1946, the Alexandra Palace came on to the air once more, and the numbers of people owning TV sets multiplied. In 1954, the Independent Television Authority was set up – making commercial TV possible. In 1967, the first colour television broadcast was made.

Once TV had become so popular, the cinema trade suffered. Many picture houses closed down. Some were adapted to a new pastime that

Into Europe

had taken the public's fancy: bingo. Perhaps everybody dreams of making a quick fortune. Those who play bingo, or else fill in football pools, obviously do.

The explosion of a nuclear bomb had been an horrific affair. Nevertheless, there was a more gentle side to this new source of energy. The British public had its first glimpse of it in 1956, when the Queen opened Calder Hall nuclear power station in Cumberland.

So much became possible; so much was explained. In 1953, the year of the Queen's Coronation, Mount Everest was climbed for the first time. One of the two men who reached the top was a New Zealander named Edmund Hillary. Four years later, Hillary, in company with the British explorer Vivian Fuchs, re-discovered the South Pole. Unlike Scott, he was able to return home to tell the story.

The 'sixties seemed to be full of new ideas. They ranged from clothes to men's hair styles to music. Groups such as the Beatles and the Rolling Stones created a new sound. It was, perhaps, more economical. Only four people were involved – which made sense in an age when high wages taxed the finances of big dance bands.

If the 1960s were an age of richness and new ideas, of a more light-hearted approach to life, the 1970s soon had a more serious story to tell. They showed that there were many problems which had not gone away; they had, so to speak, been swept under the carpet.

Ireland had been given Home Rule in 1922. Later, it became a republic. But the six counties of Northern Ireland had clung tenaciously to the UK. For those who would have preferred to see a 'united Ireland', this was bad enough. To make matters worse, the inhabitants of the six counties (or the majority of them) harboured religious prejudices against Roman Catholics. They ensured that all the top jobs went to Protestants.

As a result of riots in 1969 British troops were sent back to Northern Ireland. The riots were followed by bomb attacks, murders, and other acts of brutality, commited by Protestant and Catholic terrorist organizations. The situation worsened until, in 1972, the Northern Ireland Parliament had to be suspended, and the province was ruled directly from Westminster.

Just as the Irish question seems to be a political sickness that returns from time to time, and for which nobody seems able to find a cure, so does unemployment.

In the 1960s there appeared to be a golden age of affluence, with jobs for all and plenty of money about. The early 1970s showed that it was all a dream. The world's economics (and Britain's especially) drifted into chaos. The lines of jobless grew.

Indeed, throughout this book, you may have noticed that many of the same, or similar, problems have cropped up over and over again. There is very little that is new.

However, one area of the world has torn itself away from the past: Western Europe. After the war, Russia assembled the states of Eastern Europe into a huge Communist bloc. In 1949, alarmed about its war potential, the Western European nations – plus the United States and Canada – formed the North Atlantic Treaty Organisation (NATO) to defend themselves against attack. In military terms, at any rate, this part of the Continent was at last united.

In 1957, matters went a stage further. Under the Treaty of Rome, France, West Germany, Holland, Belgium, Luxembourg and Italy formed a European Economic Community (EEC) – otherwise known as the Common Market. The idea was to work as one nation in questions of trade and agriculture, and to eliminate all differences in taxes and customs duties.

Britain considered the idea of joining; dithered; then, in 1963, took the plunge and applied for membership. Somewhat to the negotiators' surprise, the application was rejected. General de Gaulle, then President of France and one of the most influential men in Europe, did not want the UK as a partner.

In 1967, the statesmen tried again, and again the application was turned down. At last, in 1970, Prime Minister Edward Heath made a successful attempt. But, by this time, the General was dead. Just under three years later, on 1 January, 1973, Great Britain became a full partner in the European community. The battle, there, is over – perhaps forever.

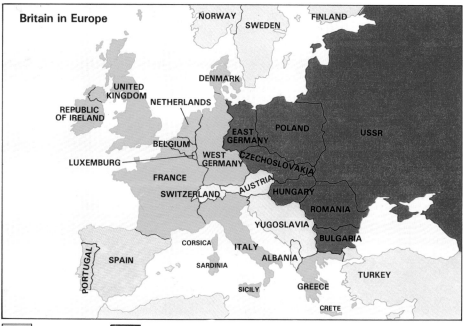

Belfast: A soldier stands guard; barbed wire forms a protective barrier; somewhere a terrorist is planning an attack.

Britain in Europe

NORWAY
SWEDEN
FINLAND
DENMARK
UNITED KINGDOM
NETHERLANDS
REPUBLIC OF IRELAND
BELGIUM
EAST GERMANY
POLAND
USSR
LUXEMBURG
WEST GERMANY
CZECHOSLOVAKIA
FRANCE
AUSTRIA
SWITZERLAND
HUNGARY
ROMANIA
YUGOSLAVIA
BULGARIA
CORSICA
ITALY
PORTUGAL
SPAIN
SARDINIA
ALBANIA
TURKEY
SICILY
GREECE
CRETE

 EEC members   The Communist Bloc
Application for membership made in 1981

Left: Britain first applied for membership of the Common Market in 1963 but was not admitted until 1970.

Imperial to Metric

Economics is all about money. In Anglo-Saxon and Norman times, they minted silver pennies known as 'sterlings'. If 240 of them were put on the scales, they weighed 1 lb – hence the expression 'one pound sterling'. As time went by, other coins were introduced: the shilling (5p), the half-crown (12½p), the golden sovereign, and so on.

Until February, 1971, they talked about British money in terms of 'pounds, shillings and pence' (or £.s.d.). But then, on a late winter's day, a lot of things changed. There had been 12 pennies to a shilling, and 20 shillings to a pound. There seemed to be neither rhyme nor reason for it – quite unlike money on the Continent, where everything was in units of 10 or 100.

And so 'decimalization' – as it was called – came to Britain. The £ remained much as it was, although worth rather less. But there were now 100 new pennies to it. The old shilling piece became worth 5p and the two-shilling piece (or florin) worth 10p. Threepenny bits, sixpenny pieces (2½p), and half-crowns were abolished. The ten shilling note was replaced by the 50p piece.

Some years later, metrication began to take over in the world of weights and measures. The result was that motorists began to buy their petrol in litres rather than gallons, and to drive for kilometres rather than miles. In the shops, kilograms gradually took over from pounds, and metres succeeded yards.

People in Europe had long been accustomed to using the metric system, and so it was hardly surprising. As members of the European community, it was sensible that we should be weighing and measuring things the same way as the other nations.

But the changes to money were not quite done. On 21 April, 1983, the pound became a coin instead of a piece of paper money. There was nothing new about this. Until the outbreak of the 1914–18 War, the pound had been represented by the golden sovereign – a coin first minted on the orders of Henry VII in 1489. But then, with gold needed for more urgent wartime purposes, pound notes were issued. A precious disc of gold was replaced by a scrap of paper.

After World War II, sovereigns were again produced by the Royal Mint, but as collectors' items rather than as money to be spent in shops. Indeed, each is worth very much more than £1. The value changes according to the price of gold, but it is usually round about £90.

The pound coins introduced in April, 1983, are manufactured from an alloy composed of 70 per cent copper – the rest is nickel and zinc. If you look at the edge, you see the words *Decus et Tutamen* inscribed on it. This is Latin for 'Ornament and Safeguard'. It was first used in 1662, during the reign of Charles II, when machines made it possible to produce sufficiently thick coins to carry such inscriptions. 'Ornament' means just what it says: a beautifully designed coin is an ornament. 'Safeguard' means that these words impose almost impossible difficulties upon counterfeiters.

The Epilogue

This book began with the earth in turmoil, taking millions of years to bring about its present mixture of land masses and oceans. The area that is now occupied by the North Sea underwent many changes. Some 250 million years ago, during one of the periods when the North Sea (today's version) actually was a sea (yesterday's version), it was inhabited by tiny living creatures – each so small, that it would have needed a microscope to see it. As time went by, these microscopic forms of life became buried beneath clay. The temperature rose: they became crushed and squeezed, and the result was a great many droplets of oil.

That, very simply, is how North Sea oil came about. The field known as Auk is between 230 and 250 million years old – probably the oldest. The origins of Brent go back roughly 170 million years; and the Forties, about 60 million years.

In 1964, when it seemed almost certain that this miracle of pre-history had created oil in the bed of the North Sea, the government issued drilling licences to oil companies. A year later, a hope became a certainty, when BP struck oil on 27 December. It was, you might say, a wonderful (if late) Christmas present for Britain.

Nowadays, the British economy depends greatly on North Sea oil. But the oil 'bonanza' was not a miracle cure for the nation's financial problems. Nearly 20 years after the first supplies came ashore, the lines of the unemployed were longer than they had ever been. The reason the politicians gave was 'world recession'. In other words, a lot of businesses in a lot of places were in a bad way. When things improved, they promised, more jobs would become available.

In fact, another industrial revolution was (and still is) taking place: a revolution just as important as that which changed the face of Britain 200 years ago. Then, it was the coming of the steam engine; now it is the development of electronics – the computer, the silicon chip, the world of 'high tech'.

Such inventions enabled man to break free from the earth's atmosphere – even to land on the moon. They came into countless homes as hi-fi, video recorders, and other things that, half a century ago, would have seemed the stuff of science fiction.

They also began to transform industry. In offices, computers became able to carry out innumerable clerical tasks – and often to do them more efficiently than people. They could direct machinery, causing it to work as a team of robots. They could, with a little help from man, even build motor cars.

With machines doing the task of humans, the need for flesh-and-blood workers began to decrease. There are, to be honest, more people than certain industries are ever likely to need again. Somehow, society will have to change. It will have to adapt itself to living with these busy mechanical brains: possibly by offering lives in which there is much more leisure. The question is: how best to use it – and how best to afford it? The answer has yet to be found.

Just as considerable economic and social problems remain to be solved, an even greater problem is the search for peace. When World War II came to an end, a lot of people hoped – even believed – that this was the last, absolutely final war. Admittedly they would have to live with the menace of nuclear weapons in the backgrounds of their lives. But this menace was so terrible, so enormous in its powers of destruction, that nobody, surely, could ever be daring enough – or mad enough – to use it. Its very existence ought to cause men to turn away from the idea of settling their quarrels by violence.

There has been no nuclear war. There have, unfortunately, been no fewer than 150 non-nuclear wars fought in various parts of the world since 1945. British troops (to mention only one nation) have been in action in Korea, Malaysia, Suez, Aden, Northern Ireland . . . and in the Falkland Islands.

During the Falklands campaign, the social and economic woes of Britain, were pushed to the backs of many people's minds. Even in parliament, the rival parties came unusually close to agreeing with one another. Perhaps it requires a war to unite a nation. If so, it is a pity: there must be better ways. To find them may be the challenge of those who read this book.

Right: In 1965 oil was discovered beneath the North Sea. Now Britain produces more oil than it consumes, a vital factor for a highly industrialized nation. But even the 'gift' of oil leaves many economic problems to be solved.

The Monarchy Today

The rulers of Britain have had a chequered career: they have been feared, adored, ridiculed, and in one case publicly executed.

Today the monarchy seems more popular than ever. This is partly as a result of the fairy-tale romance between Charles, Prince of Wales, and his bride, which captured the imagination of the people.

Britain had long been wondering whom the Prince would marry. Then on 24 February, 1981, the news broke: he had become engaged to Lady Diana Spencer. On 29 July, 1981, they were married in St Paul's Cathedral amid a blaze of pageantry. They continue to prove that the monarchy is far from being a thing of the past.

Important and Interesting Dates

500,000BC	Stone Age man probably existed in Britain
12,000BC	The last of the Ice Ages recedes
5,000BC	Strait of Dover formed; England cut off from Continent
2000BC	Beaker Folk arrive from Europe; Bronze Age begins
1800BC	Work starts on building Stonehenge
500BC	Iron Age begins as first Celts arrive from Europe
55BC	Caesar's first expedition to Britain
AD43	Romans occupy the British Isles
AD60	Boadicea leads uprising
406	Roman legions leave Britain; withdraw to Rome
449	Invasion of Kent by Hengist and Horsa
597	Augustine brings return of Christianity to England
851	Danish forces occupy much of Britain
871	Alfred becomes King of Wessex; in 878, he defeats Danish leader Guthrum
1014	Saxon King Ethelred (the 'Unready') flees to Normandy; Danish King Cnut occupies throne
1042	Ethelred's son, Edward the Confessor, returns to England from Normandy; is crowned King
1066	Norman invasion; King Harold killed at Battle of Hastings
1087	Death of William I (the 'Conqueror')
1093	Malcolm III of Scotland invades England; is killed at Alnwick
1135	Stephen of Boulogne siezes English throne; breakdown of law and order
1170	**Thomas Becket murdered in Canterbury Cathedral**
1191	Richard I departs for Holy Land on his crusade
1215	King John forced by Barons to sign Magna Carta
1284	Wales overcome by English; divided into counties in the English style
1295	Edward I summons the 'Model Parliament' – the beginning of the present system of parliamentary government
1296	Edward I affronts Scots by removing Coronation Stone from Scone to Westminster Abbey
1298	Wallace defeated by Edward I at Stirling (executed in London seven years later)
1306	Scots revolt under Robert Bruce
1337	Beginning of Hundred Years War
1338	Light cannon first mounted on warships
1343	Gold florins (value: 30p each) introduced to coinage
1348	Outbreak of Black Death
1352	First evidence of spectacles being worn
1370	Steel crossbows first used by soldiers
1381	Peasants' Revolt
1453	Hundred Years War ends with French victory at Castillon (English victories included Sluys – 1340, Crecy – 1346, and Agincourt – 1415).
1455	Wars of the Roses begin at the Battle of St Albans
1460	Barbers are taught to become dentists
1461	Gunpowder manufactured in the Tower of London
1476	Caxton sets up his printing press in London
1483	Richard of Gloucester proclaims himself Richard III; the young King Edward V and his brother, Richard of York, vanish mysteriously in the Tower of London
1485	Richard III defeated and killed at Battle of Bosworth. Henry Tudor (Henry VII) becomes king
1489	+ (for addition) − (for subtraction) signs first used in arithmetic
1499	Perkin Warbeck, confidence trickster and pretender to the throne, executed after attempting to escape from the Tower
1517	Martin Luther in Germany proclaims Protestantism and starts the Reformation
1533	Henry VIII declares himself head of the church in England
1536	Anne Boleyn executed; dissolution of the monasteries begins
1551	First coach is used in Britain
1564	William Shakespeare born (first plays performed in 1592)
1568	Mary Queen of Scots flees to England; imprisoned (executed in 1587)
1577	Francis Drake sets off on his voyage around the world
1579	First atlas of Britain published
1585	Earliest English spring-driven clock still in existence manufactured
1588	Defeat of Spanish Armada
1590	First paper mill in Britain established at Dartford in Kent
1592	Bow and arrow finally abandoned as a weapon of war
1596	Water closet installed at Richmond Palace (but not generally used until two centuries later)
1603	Death of Queen Elizabeth I; James VI of Scotland becomes James I of England
1605	Gunpowder Plot discovered
1616	Death of William Shakespeare
1620	Pilgrim Fathers sail for America in Mayflower
1625	First use of fire engines in England
1628	Earl of Buckingham murdered by John Felton
1635	Postal services between London and Edinburgh introduced
1640	Short Parliament sits April–May; later in year, Long Parliament assembled
1641	Court of Star Chamber abolished by Parliament
1642	Charles I attempts to arrest five MPs; later in year, first battle of the Civil War is fought at Edge Hill
1644	Battle of Marston Moor leads to formation of the New Model Army (by Roundheads) – turning point of Civil War
1645	Battle of Naseby
1646	Charles I surrenders to Scots (who hand him over to Parliament in 1647 for £400,000)
1649	Trial and execution of Charles I
1653	Dutch fleet defeated off Portland
1657	Oliver Cromwell refuses title of king Fountain pens first manufactured (in Paris)
1658	Oliver Cromwell dies; succeeded as Lord Protector by his son
1660	Charles II restored to throne
1665	Great Plague causes many deaths in London
1666	Fire of London
1667	Milton publishes *Paradise Lost*

1678	Titus Oates claims to have discovered 'Popish Plot'
1685	Duke of Monmouth lands in West Country; defeated at Sedgemoor
1688	William III of Orange lands at Torbay
1690	James II defeated by William III's army at Battle of the Boyne in Ireland
1692	Massacre of Glencoe
1694	Bank of England founded
1700	*Vox Stellarum* (later *Old Moore's Almanack*) first published
1702	The *Daily Courant*, Britain's first newspaper, introduced; War of Spanish Succession breaks out
1706	First insurance company (the Hand-in-Hand) formed
1707	Act of Union causes England and Scotland to be governed by the same parliament
1711	Thomas Newcomen builds first steam engine – for pumping water out of mines
1712	Last execution for witchcraft in England
1720	South Sea Bubble bursts Wallpaper used in Britain for first time
1739	Outbreak of War of Jenkins Ear John Wesley founds Methodists
1745	Prince Charles leads Jacobite rebellion (the 'Forty-Five'), which (in 1746) ends in disaster at Culloden
1759	General Wolfe takes Quebec
1760	Botanical Gardens opened at Kew
1773	The Boston Tea Party – American colonists protest against the duty on tea
1776	American Declaration of Independence; beginning of the American War of Independence, which ends with Cornwallis's defeat at Yorktown in 1781
1789	French Revolution – followed, in 1793, by war between Britain and France
1801	*Charlotte Dundas*, the first steamer, demonstrated in the Clyde
1805	Battle of Trafalgar; death of Nelson
1812	First Luddite Riots
1815	Defeat of Napoleon at Waterloo
1829	First police force in Britain established by Sir Robert Peel
1830	Liverpool–Manchester Railway opened
1834	Slavery abolished in all British possessions Six farm labourers from Tolpuddle in Dorset (the 'Tolpuddle Martyrs') transported for trying to form a trade union Hansom cab (a two-wheeler) invented
1840	Queen Victoria marries Prince Albert
1843	SS *Great Britain* (3,500 tons) becomes first screw-driven steamship to enter North Atlantic service
1851	Great Exhibition
1854	Outbreak of Crimean War; charge of Light Brigade at Balaclava
1855	First iron-built Cunarder crosses Atlantic in 9½ days
1857	Indian Mutiny
1858	Big Ben (named after Sir Benjamin Hall), the 13½-ton bell of the Houses of Parliament, cast at a foundry in London's Whitechapel
1885	General Gordon killed at Khartoum First electric tramcar comes into service (at Blackpool)

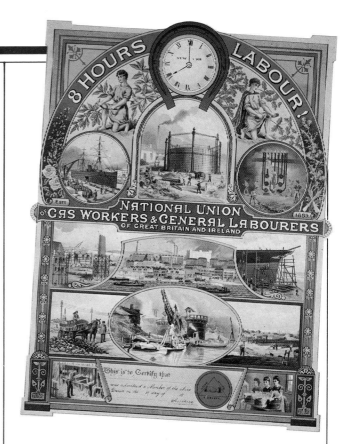

1899	Outbreak of Boer War
1901	First British submarine built
1906	First Rolls-Royce manufactured
1912	*Titanic* (acclaimed as the world's greatest liner) sinks after colliding with an iceberg on her maiden voyage
1914	Assassination of Austrian Archduke Franz Ferdinand; outbreak of First World War
1916	Easter rising in Dublin First tank (*Little Willie*) used in battle First air raids on London
1919	Treaty of Versailles First non-stop flight across the Atlantic
1922	First radio entertainment broadcast
1925	First TV set manufactured
1926	General Strike
1928	Penicillin discovered by Sir Alexander Fleming
1929	Beginning of economic slump
1936	January: Edward VIII becomes King on death of George V; December: Edward VIII abdicates
1939	Outbreak of Second World War
1940	Evacuation at Dunkirk; Battle of Britain; beginning of the Blitz
1944	Allied invasion of Normandy (D-Day); first kidney machine built
1945	Explosion of atomic bombs in Japan brings Second World War to an end
1946	National Health Service introduced
1947	Break-up of British Empire begins with granting independence to India
1951	Festival of Britain
1952	Death of George VI; Queen Elizabeth II comes to the throne
1965	Crude oil discovered in the bed of the North Sea
1969	Maiden flight of *Concorde*; maiden voyage of *QE2*
1971	Decimal currency replaces the old system of £ s d
1973	Britain enters Common Market
1982	Falklands conflict between Britain and Argentina

141

Index

Photographic Acknowledgements

Aerofilms 6, 7, 39; Archeological Museum, Hull 15 (top); Ashmolean Museum Photographic Services 25 (top); Bridgeman Art Library 20 (left), 33, 35, 48 (bottom left), 51, 53 (right), 54 (top), 57, 61, 85, 92, 93 (middle), 94, 96 (bottom), 98, 104, 110 (bottom), 112, 125 (top); BBC Hulton Picture Library 81 (left), 87 (bottom right), 100 (top), 101, 102 (bottom right), 107, 108 (bottom left), 115 (top left and right), 116 (left), 117, 120, 126 (bottom), 127 (right), 128 (top and bottom), 133; British Aerospace 134 (top); British Film Institute 127 (left); British Museum 10, 14 (top), 16, 48 (bottom left); British Tourist Authority 14 (bottom), 18, 28, 34, 113; Daily Telegraph Colour Library 138 (bottom); E.T. Archive 8 (top and bottom), 91 (top), 132 (bottom); Fotomas Index 19, 31 (top), 43 (top), 46, 49, 50 (top), 53 (left); 59 (top), 73 (top), 76 (bottom). 78, 81 (top right), 84, 88 (left, 91 (bottom), 93 (bottom), 102 (top left and right), 108 (right), 141; Greater London Council 90; Michael Holford 9, 63; Robert Hunt 129, 130; Imperial War Museum 111 (top right and bottom left), 125 (bottom), 126 (top); A. F. Kersting 25 (bottom); Mobil Oil 139; The Mansell Collection 2, 55, 74 (top), 79, 80, 82 (bottom), 93 (top), 96 (top), 115 (middle left); Mary Evans Picture Library 26, 43 (bottom), 100 (bottom), 106, 114; National Portrait Gallery 42, 48 (top right), 59 (bottom), 60, 73 (bottom), 75 (top left), 82 (middle), 88 (bottom right), 95 (top), 105 (bottom right), 118 (bottom); Orbis Publishing Library 131 (bottom), 132 (top); Popperfoto 136 (bottom); Public Record Office 30; Peter Roberts 37, 44 (top), 45; Royal Geographical Society 135; Scottish Development Department 11; Universitetets Oldsaksamling, Oslo 20 (bottom right); Vogue © Conde Nast, from *The Art of Vogue Covers*, Octopus Books Ltd. 128 (middle).